Country

The Life, Times, & Music Series

Country
The Life, Times, & Music Series

Peter O.E. Bekker, Jr.

Consulting Editor for the Life, Times, & Music Series
Peter O.E. Bekker, Jr.

Friedman/Fairfax Publishers

ISBN 1-56799-044-4

THE LIFE, TIMES, & MUSIC SERIES: COUNTRY
was prepared and produced by
Michael Friedman Publishing Group, Inc.
15 West 26th Street
New York, New York, 10010

Editor: Nathaniel Marunas
Art Director: Jeff Batzli
Designer: Susan E. Livingston
Photography Editor: Jennifer Crowe McMichael
Consulting Editor: Peter O.E. Bekker, Jr.

Printed in the United States of America

For bulk purchases and special sales, please contact:
Friedman/Fairfax Publishers
15 West 26 Street
New York, NY 10010
(212) 685-6610 FAX (212) 685-1307

Contents

Introduction

The story of country music is partly a story of business. It is a familiar story in the United States, a tale of entrepreneurs who stumbled upon a product, developed it, nurtured and fine-tuned it, and skillfully created markets to cash in big on it. But it is also a more profound story, a tale of roots and family, of cul-

ture clashes and festering resent-

ments, and the process of change.

It is a story of the comforts of nos-

talgia, and the often harsh light of

day. For many Americans, country

music is a diary of the United States

growing up.

Opposite page: Johnny Cash, a worldly
expression on his face even then, poses
at the tender age of twenty-six with his
custom-made guitar. Above: Alan
Jackson is one of the many contemporary artists who are breathing new life
into country music. Left: Crystal Gayle
is one of the smooth country performers
who prospered during the 1980s.

Publicity photo for WLS Radio's "Barn Dance of the Air," later called The National Barn Dance, *showing a good old-fashioned hoedown.*

Country music's roots are in folk and traditional music and its appeal has always been its simplicity and sincerity, but as it exists today it is also the product of years of commercialization that has shaped, spun, and transformed a down-home craft into a booming global industry.

Deftly adjusted over the years to accommodate changing times and changing tastes, country music is now the fastest-growing radio format, a popular vehicle for advertisers, and a gleaming, seemingly bottomless mother lode for record companies. It offers a dizzying assortment of styles designed to appeal to the widest possible audience, styles that include contemporary, traditional, new traditional, country rock, and country soul.

In 1924, George D. Hay, hungry for programming material like all radio broadcasters, launched a "Barn Dance of the Air" on radio station WLS in Chicago, inviting fiddle players and string bands into the WLS studios to play pretty much whatever they could. His program was immediately successful and was quickly imitated by other stations around the country. As a folksy character called the "Solemn Ol' Judge," Hay emceed the WLS show and a subsequent, equally historic broadcast in Nashville, Tennessee, called the Grand Ole Opry. The man who put country music on the map spent the remainder of his career trying to maintain the down-home, traditional flavor of the music and the musicians who appeared under his auspices. This was a battle he eventually lost to changing times and the pursuit of profit.

Roy Acuff (seen here in a 1943 performance with the Smoky Mountain Boys) was a mainstay on the Grand Ole Opry for most of his long career.

George D. Hay (1895–1968) and the Grand Ole Opry

It was a newspaperman from Indiana who founded, built, and shaped the Grand Ole Opry, country music's most prestigious stage and a radio broadcast that in more than sixty years has featured every great name in the field.

George Dewey Hay was in his early twenties when he moved from his hometown of Attica, Indiana, to Memphis, Tennessee, to take a reporting job on the *Memphis Commercial Appeal* newspaper. At the time, commercial radio was in its infancy, and the *Memphis Appeal*, like many newspapers, had invested in a station of its own, mostly as a tool to sell newspapers. Fascinated by the new medium, Hay took a job as an announcer while continuing to work as a reporter. Soon afterward, having established himself in radio and deciding he liked the work, Hay moved to Chicago, where he was hired as an announcer by WLS, a 50,000-watt powerhouse whose signal still blankets most of the Midwest.

Programming in those early days was hard to come by. Records were played, but there were not many of them. Skits were performed, and those were usually popular. Mostly, radio was a medium for lengthy commercial announcements by a station's owner, or a particular program's sponsor.

One day an idea was hatched at WLS to invite amateur musicians into the studio for a "Barn Dance of the Air." Those live concerts gobbled up quite a few hours of broadcast time, and soon the barn dances could be heard morning, noon, and night. Public reaction was immediately favorable and, because of its powerful signal, the nighttime barn dance show on WLS was quickly renamed *The National Barn Dance*, and Hay was installed as master of ceremonies. Not particularly musical, Hay played no instruments, and never sang or wrote a song. But he had always loved the informal hoedowns that were put on by local pickers in the Ozark mountains,

and in other places he traveled. He was tremendously impressed with the energy of the music and the joy that it brought the players and their audiences. He was the perfect choice for ringmaster of the WLS program.

It was on *The National Barn Dance* that Hay began developing the "Solemn Ol' Judge" character that later became his signature as host of the Grand Ole Opry. The Chicago show featured string bands, square-dance callers, and fiddlers, and it eventually branched out to include "singing cowboys" such as Gene Autry. As time went by, mainstream pop singers and balladeers were also featured. Much later, WLS became one of the first stations to adopt the records-only Top 40 format, and *The National Barn Dance* moved to another Chicago powerhouse, WGN, remaining on the air there until 1968.

Hay hosted *The National Barn Dance* only until 1925. As the Solemn Ol' Judge, he blew a steamboat whistle to kick off each segment of the program and otherwise did his best to assure that the folksy, "barn dance" flavor was maintained.

An offer from the National Life and Accident Insurance Company lured Hay to Nashville in 1925. The firm owned WSM there, a low-power station with a fifty-mile range, and Hay was hired to run it. At first it seemed like a step down. Nashville was a much smaller city than Chicago and WSM was a tiny station compared to WLS, which could also be heard in Nashville, hundreds of miles from Chicago. But Hay was inspired by the challenge of directing the new station and one of his first suggestions was for a barn dance program like the one he had emceed in Chicago. It was not an easy sell, for the station's owners were hoping for a more sophisticated image, but Hay ultimately prevailed.

The *WSM Barn Dance* went on the air on November 28, 1925. The Solemn Ol' Judge held forth as master of ceremonies, but

it was an unspectacular debut. The only performer on the maiden broadcast was an elderly fiddler named Uncle Jimmy Thompson who despite his age did his best to entertain. Within weeks, however, WSM was deluged with requests from local amateurs for a shot at some radio time. Hay would anoint the performers with down-home names like the Possum Hunters or the Clod Hoppers.

WSM carried a number of programs, including a New York City classical music broadcast that sometimes preceded the *Barn Dance*. It is said that one night as he opened his show, Hay bellowed, "Folks, you've been up in the clouds with grand opera...now get down to earth with us...in a shindig of Grand Ole Opry!" Whether or not that story is true, by 1926 the WSM show was being called the Grand Ole Opry.

WSM raised its power to 50,000 watts in 1932. With its signal loud and clear throughout the Mississippi Valley, along the East Coast, and into Canada, the influence of

the broadcast grew significantly. The vigilant Hay continued to serve as master of ceremonies until 1956, determined that the Opry remain true to its roots as down-home, folksy entertainment. The show stretched to three hours in length, and portions of it were networked to the nation over NBC. As the Opry grew in stature, its importance to the increasingly powerful Nashville music industry also grew. Its homespun appeal couldn't last. During the late 1950s, the Opry was transformed into a slick, structured showcase for Nashville's burgeoning music machine.

Hay retired to Virginia, returning to Nashville in 1966, ten years after leaving the Opry, to be inducted into the Country Music Hall of Fame. His death on May 9, 1968, was announced first over WSM in a special tribute to one of the station's earliest employees and the founder of the longest-running program on American radio, a national institution that can still be heard every Saturday from Nashville.

In 1925 Hay convinced the National Life and Accident Insurance Company, owners of radio station WSM in Nashville, to broadcast a show called the Grand Ole Opry. The Opry would soon become the premier venue for country's top performers, and Nashville would become their mecca. But in 1925, Nashville was just a capital city and "barn dance" music was very much the purview of hillbillies.

Roots

The barn dance broadcasts on WLS, WSM, and the many other radio stations that adopted the idea featured mostly amateur players who performed folk tunes and traditional music. These were usually folk songs of the British Isles that had made their way to faraway shores in the hearts and minds of settlers who played, sang, and handed them down for centuries, mostly in the rural isolation of homesteads and small towns of the pre-industrial United States. In those days, before the advent of mass media and near-effortless transportation, entertainment was mostly homespun, with sing-alongs and community music-making high on the short list of diversions.

Music was performed by individuals or by small string bands, usually some combination of fiddle, guitar, Dobro, autoharp, and double bass. It was very common for music to be the accompaniment to any group activity, for example, barn raisings, hog slaughterings, harvests, and so on. Tent shows and fiddler's conventions were also popular musical events; they served as both entertainments and competitions, and provided an opportunity for isolated people to gather together and socialize.

The twenties were an important time in the development not only of country music, but also of blues and jazz. Not surprisingly, the blues guitar innovations of black musicians were finding their way out of the Mississippi Delta and into the mountains of Appalachia. The couriers were minstrels, sharecroppers, and other itinerants, and it wasn't unusual to hear black and white string bands adopting elements of each other's music.

Impromptu sing-alongs and musical "jams" were important social and recreational outlets for settlers and homesteaders.

Jimmie Rodgers (1897–1933), "The Father of Country Music"

A young, white Mississippian named Jimmie Rodgers was deeply influenced by the blues. A supernova on the early country scene, Rodgers had a brief but brilliant career that established the appeal of country music without any doubt; furthermore, his musical dexterity was an inspiration to nearly every country performer who followed.

Discovered in 1927 by New York record executive Ralph Peer, who was on a talent hunt in the South, Jimmie Rodgers had already been performing professionally for two years, as a banjo player in a blackface troupe and as leader of a group called the Jimmie Rodgers Entertainers.

Sickly and slight, Rodgers would eventually die of tuberculosis at a young age. Incredibly, his career as a musician spanned only eight years, but his fame was such that he inspired thousands of imitators and became country's first superstar. Rodgers is remembered as a pioneer who incorporated nearly every style of popular music into his performances, and because of that, he is credited with founding the commercial school of country music, a branch that had immense impact on the later emergence of honky tonk, rockabilly, and rock and roll. Later luminaries as diverse as Gene Autry, Ernest Tubb, Hank Williams, Lefty Frizzell, Howlin' Wolf (1910–1976), B.B. King (1925–   ), Merle Haggard, and Willie Nelson have all acknowledged their debt to Rodgers.

The son of a railroad worker, Rodgers was born on September 8, 1897, in Meridian, Mississippi. He left school in 1911 to work with his father on the railroad, laboring for the Mobile and Ohio Line as a waterboy, callboy, and brakeman. He picked up an extensive musical repertoire in his travels, and learned the rudiments of banjo and guitar from some of the black laborers to whom he brought water. Ill health forced his retirement from railroad work in 1924, and he began his new career in music almost immediately.

The Jimmie Rodgers Entertainers met with modest success and even managed to land a regular spot playing dance music on an Asheville, North

Carolina, radio station. Responding to an advertisement placed by Ralph Peer, Rodgers traveled to Bristol, Virginia, in 1927, to audition for Peer's label, Victor Records. His band did not come along, and Rodgers kept the date as a soloist, accompanying himself on guitar.

Jimmie Rodgers, the "Blue Yodeler," was country's first international superstar.

The Bristol Sessions

Held in a warehouse in which Peer had set up a makeshift recording studio, the Bristol sessions were a defining moment for country music. Besides Rodgers, one of the many acts who showed up was a trio from nearby Maces Springs, Virginia, called the Carter Family.

A.P., Sara, and Maybelle Carter made the thirty-mile trip to sing a selection of traditional folk and mountain tunes for Peer, among them "Poor Orphan Child" and "Single Girl, Married Girl." Immediately impressed with Sara Carter's haunting voice and Maybelle Carter's distinctive guitar style, Peer paid the family fifty dollars per song. Two days later, Peer made Jimmie Rodgers a similar offer after hearing him sing "Sleep, Baby, Sleep" and "The Soldier's Sweetheart."

None of the tunes recorded by Peer during the Bristol sessions sold particularly well, but because of the discovery of the Carter Family and Jimmie Rodgers, the sessions are now seen as the historical wellspring of contemporary country music. These acts formed the musical river from which country's many tributaries would later flow. The Carters pioneered and prac-

Hoping to cash in on the "hillbilly music" craze, record company executive Ralph Peer "discovered" such seminal country artists as Jimmie Rodgers and the Original Carter Family.

Country music's founders in a rare group photo taken in Louisville, Kentucky. Left to right: Jimmie Rodgers, Maybelle Carter, A.P. Carter, Sara Carter.

ticed the conservative, traditional style, while Rodgers, eclectic to the core, was the inspiration for the cowboy, honky-tonk, outlaw, country-rock, and country-soul derivatives.

A little more than a month after his audition in Bristol, Rodgers went up to New York City to lobby Peer for more recording sessions. While there, he recorded "Blue Yodel Number One (T is for Texas)" and it became an immediate hit, launching his brief, brilliant, historic career.

Rodgers recorded about one hundred songs in all. He was in big demand for concerts but his poor health limited his touring schedule and the length of time he was able to spend on stage. Audiences appreciated his folksy self-effacement and did not begrudge his flamboyance, even in the throes of the Great Depression. Listeners were aware of his frailty and if anything, songs like "T.B. Blues" and "Whippin' That Old T.B." further endeared him to them.

In the end, though, Rodgers was not able to beat tuberculosis. He died at New York's Taft Hotel on May 26, 1933, soon after completing another recording session for Ralph Peer. The nation mourned for the "Blue Yodeler" and more than a few songs of tribute to him became hits. When the Country Music Hall of Fame was created in 1961, Jimmie Rodgers was the first performer to be inducted.

The Original Carter Family

They sang of an America that was quickly disappearing in the glitter and clamor of the Roaring Twenties. Their unadorned, traditional music enshrined the unadorned, traditional lives of the rural homesteaders and small-town Americans whose stories they told. Their catalog of more than three hundred recorded songs is a historic, living record of the American folk tradition—it is the foundation of country music as we know it today.

Alvin Pleasant Delaney Carter (1891–1960) was born in mid-December in Maces Springs in the Clinch Mountain area of western Virginia. One of Robert and Mollie Carter's nine children, A.P. was raised on heavy doses of both music and religion. As a young man, he could be heard singing in local church quartets, his tremulous bass voice strengthening into the instrument that would become familiar to millions.

A.P. Carter married Sara Dougherty (1898–1979) in 1915, and the pair settled near Maces Springs. They would sing and play music as the spirit moved them, Sara's autoharp, banjo, or guitar providing the rhythm that supported her strong alto voice and A.P.'s bass. It wasn't unusual for Sara and A.P. to entertain neighbors with the songs they had "worked up," mostly traditional folk songs or folk song variations. Sara's cousin Maybelle Addington (1909–1978) would occasionally contribute a guitar part, intriguing listeners with her unusual way of playing a bass line with her thumb while at the same time strumming a rhythm with the backs of her fingertips. Maybelle sometimes embellished her playing with occasional grace notes, a technique that came to be called the "Carter scratch," a breakthrough in the use of the guitar and an inspiration to countless future players.

The Carter scratch might very well have been known as the "Addington scratch" if Maybelle hadn't married A.P.'s brother, Ezra, in 1926. But it's more likely that no one would have remembered Maybelle's innovation at all if, the very next year, the trio hadn't made the thirty-mile drive to Bristol, Virginia, to audition for Ralph Peer of Victor Records, who was offering fifty dollars a song; that kind of money was not easy to come by in the hardscrabble hills of Virginia.

Peer was immediately impressed with the Carters and bought six of their numbers for the advertised price of fifty dollars each. Giddy from the excitement of the audition and especially from their three-hundred-dollar windfall, the Carters returned to their homes and resumed their lives as homesteaders.

Several months passed before Ralph Peer contacted A.P. to invite the Carters up to Camden, New Jersey, for another recording session. The 1928 trip resulted in the release of "Wildwood Flower," and "Keep on the Sunny Side," two of the family's best-known songs. Peer generously upped his purchase price to seventy-five dollars per song for the Camden sessions, and while Victor Records was doing very well selling the Carters' music, the family received no royalties.

It was A.P.'s habit to scour the hills around Maces Springs, looking for material. He would visit his neighbors, and make long treks to distant parts, searching for songs or stories to put to music. Much of what the Carters recorded, like "Will the Circle be Unbroken," is authentic folk or traditional music. Since many of the folk tunes had been jumbled in their journey through time, A.P. would often rewrite lyrics, or compose his own. Sara and Maybelle worked up the arrangements, and the three together would negotiate how the material would be performed. Even if their renditions were hybrid, the Carters maintained a vocal and instrumental integrity in their music that endeared them to millions of listeners who, during the Great Depression, found their dreams shattered.

The Carter Sisters and Mother Maybelle carried on the Carter Family's legacy after the Original Carter Family dissolved. Left to right: Helen, Maybelle, Anita.

The success of their records put the Carter Family on the road, and they performed as a unit until 1943, most successfully after a three-year stint on XERA, a "border radio" station in Mexico, just across the line from Del Rio, Texas. American law limited the power of radio stations to 50,000 watts but XERA broadcast at an unprecedented 500,000 watts, blanketing most of the United States with its signal.

In later years, country talents from Waylon Jennings and Chet Atkins (1924–) to George Jones and Woody Guthrie (1912–1967) would tell of listening to the Carter Family over XERA. Atkins was especially impressed with Maybelle's scratch, and Guthrie, too, learned to imitate her guitar style. Guthrie wrote the lyrics to two of his most famous songs over Carter Family melodies: "Reuben James" (based on "Wildwood Flower"), and "This Land Is Your Land" (based on "Darling Pal of Mine").

A.P. and Sara Carter separated in 1933. Even though they lived apart, the Carter Family continued to appear together until Sara moved to California in 1942 with her new husband, A.P.'s cousin, Coy Bayes.

In the fifties, a brief attempt at a comeback that included their children, Joe and Janette Carter, fizzled, and in 1956 they again retired, neither of them to perform professionally again.

Maybelle and her three daughters, June, Helen, and Anita, continued on the performance trail as The Carter Sisters and Mother Maybelle. In a few years they were the toast of Nashville, becoming regulars on the Grand Ole Opry in 1950. In 1961, June Carter joined Johnny Cash's (1932–) wildly popular "Road Show," and as the folk revival movement of that decade gathered momentum, Cash hired Maybelle, Anita, and Helen as well. The family made regular appearances on Cash's national television show in the sixties, and June, after divorcing country singer Carl Smith, married Cash in 1968.

A.P. Carter's heart failed on November 7, 1960, in Maces Springs; Mother Maybelle died on October 23, 1978, in Madison, Tennessee; and Sara died a short time later, in Lodi, California, on January 8, 1979.

Fulfilling a promise she made to her dying father in 1960, Janette Carter set up a small theater near Maces Springs called the Fold, where the family's music is regularly performed; from time to time, Carter descendants, illustrious in their own right, can sometimes be heard leading gatherings of local folk and the curious in songs that have since become country music anthems.

Nostalgia for the Wild West, as exemplified by this frontier dance hall, helped popularize the "singing cowboys" of the 1930s.

The Singing Cowboys

Things happened quickly in country music at about the same time as the Great Depression swept the nation. In 1930, a little-known singer from Tioga, Texas, named Gene Autry (1907–   ) began appearing on WLS in Chicago as a "singing cowboy." Autry was not a cowboy, but he crooned tunes about the prairie, the range, and the wild, wild West, and he quickly became a sensation. Thanks to the shrewd sales force at Chicago-based Sears and Roebuck, he also became a huge merchandising vehicle for a full line of cowboy items, from saddles to Gene Autry guitars.

Westerns were the rage in Hollywood at the time, and Autry swiftly made his way there, parlaying his radio success into an immensely profitable career in the movies, and later, in television. A posse of other western singer-actors, including Roy Rogers, Tex Ritter, Rex Allen, Johnny Bond, and Monte Hale, soon sprang up. (John Wayne may have been the first cowboy to sing in a movie. As a character named Singin' Sandy Saunders in the 1933 film *Riders of Destiny*, Wayne self-consciously warbles a tune just before gunning down a villain.)

Cowboys (especially singing cowboys) were firmly entrenched in American pop culture during the thirties and forties even though very few of the silver screen crooners had ever done a day's work on the range. Mostly, the music of Hollywood's singing cowboys was not authentic. It had nothing to do with the songs sung in the late 1800s by real cowboys who entertained themselves around the campfire and in their bunkhouses with, among other things, music-making. By contrast, the music of Hollywood's hopalongs was professionally composed, strictly for commercial purposes; this music enhanced scenes in movie westerns, advanced the careers of their singers, and earned saddlebags of money for everyone involved.

A fourth-generation Texan, Woodward Maurice "Tex" Ritter became the epitome of the Hollywood cowboy. He appeared on Broadway, starred in more than sixty westerns, and had hits with such songs as "Get Along, Little Dogies," and "Jingle Jangle, Jingle."

Gene Autry is given official credit as Hollywood's first singing cowboy for his vocal performances in the 1934 movie *In Old Sante Fe*. The producers brought him out from Chicago to sing several campfire songs. Ken Maynard, an authentic ex-cowboy, was the movie's star. Autry followed that appearance with a thirteen-episode serialized western called *Phantom Empire*, and in 1935 appeared in *Tumbling Tumbleweeds*. During his film career, Autry made almost one hundred movies; in the late 1930s he was one of Hollywood's highest-grossing movie stars.

Following World War II, Autry continued that success on television, and later in life made a successful transition to the world of business, where he invested profitably in real estate, television and radio stations, and the California Angels baseball team. One of his foundations built and operates the Gene Autry Western Heritage Museum in Los Angeles.

In 1942, Autry's movie mantle passed to Roy Rogers (1912–   ), who emerged from the now-legendary cowboy singing group The Sons of the Pioneers, which he had cofounded in the mid-1930s with his friend Bob Nolan (1908–1980), author of the classic western tune "Tumblin' Tumbleweeds,"

Hollywood's first "singing cowboy," Gene Autry parlayed his talents into successful careers in radio, movies, records, television, and business.

The Sons of the Pioneers made movie appearances and released several records, but only Roy Rogers (not pictured here) went on to become a movie and television star in his own right.

among many others. Rogers had also made brief appearances in several westerns, including *Tumbling Tumbleweeds.* It wasn't until the mid-forties, however, that Rogers became known as "The King of the Cowboys." In 1947 he married "The Queen of the West," Dale Evans (1912–   ), and the two of them—accompanied by Rogers' famous horse, Trigger, and their dog, Bullet—rode, roped, and sang their way to superstardom.

Like Autry, Rogers and Evans also had tremendous success on television, and it was Dale Evans who wrote their television show's nostalgic theme song, "Happy Trails." The best estimate of the pair's merchandising appeal is that by the end of their active careers, the names Roy Rogers and Dale Evans were associated with some fifteen thousand products.

Autry, Rogers, and the other singing cowboys had at least as much impact on attire as they did on music. Many non-cowboy country performers began appearing in Hollywood-style cowboy hats and cowboy boots, probably to cash in on the popularity of their movie star cousins. And it was in the thirties that the words "country" and "western" got hooked together for the first time in a term that was inaccurate as a description, but was nevertheless preferred to the much more unflattering "hillbilly music."

Cowboy music flourished for about twenty years. The last singing cowboy movies were made in the early fifties. But during the period of cowboy music's popularity, nearly everyone got into the act. Bing Crosby had hits with "Home on the Range," "Tumbling Tumbleweeds," and "I'm An Old Cowhand (From the Rio Grande)," the last of which was written by Johnny Mercer, who was as far removed from the cowboy as it is possible to be. Even the ultimate sophisticate, Cole Porter, cashed in with "Don't Fence Me In." Other pop singers also embraced wild West themes: Dinah Shore had a hit with "Buttons and Bows," Frankie Laine recorded "Mule Train," and Vaughn Monroe's "Ghost Riders in the Sky" was a tremendous success.

Patsy Montana became the first woman to sell a million records in 1935 with "I Want to Be a Cowboy's Sweetheart." At about that time in Texas, Gene Autry's native state, fiddle player Bob Wills began carving out a more sophisticated brand of cowboy music that came to be called western swing.

As "King of the Cowboys" and "Queen of the West," Roy Rogers and Dale Evans became the nation's favorite sweethearts of the rodeo.

Patsy Montana (1912–   )

The first female country music star and the first woman to sell one million records as a solo performer, Patsy Montana was born Ruby Blevins near Hot Springs, Arkansas, on October 30, 1912, the only daughter in a family with eleven children.

Fascinated with cowboy music at an early age, Blevins taught herself to sing and yodel like her radio favorites. She later took up the violin as a college student at the University of the West (now the University of California at Los Angeles).

She formed an all-female singing group in the late twenties, calling it the Montana Cowgirls. The trio appeared at small events and on radio shows, and it was with the Cowgirls that Blevins changed her name to Patsy Montana.

Montana achieved wider recognition in 1933 when she joined the Prairie Ramblers, a male quartet that appeared on big-time radio shows, including *The National Barn Dance* on Chicago's WLS. The singing cowboy craze was just beginning in those years, and the Prairie Ramblers remained a very popular act until the end of the 1940s. It was during her years with the Ramblers that Montana had her historic success with "I Wanna Be a Cowboy's Sweetheart" (1935). She also appeared in a number of serial westerns with Gene Autry.

Montana followed "Cowboy's Sweetheart" with a number of similar, but less successful songs, including "Sweetheart of the Saddle" (1936), "There's a Ranch in the Sky" (1937), "Singing in the Saddle" (1939), and "Shy Little Ann from Cheyenne" (1940).

Bob Wills (1905–1975)

One of country music's great innovators, Bob Wills became known as "The King of Western Swing" during his long career. He incorporated jazz and blues motifs in a swirling, danceable mix of bluegrass and Texas folk music, pioneering country's Austin, Texas, branch of music. He directly influenced such outlaw musicians as Merle Haggard, Roger Miller (1936–1993), and Willie Nelson.

Wills did not invent western swing but he and his bands, especially the Texas Playboys, indisputably popularized it. Wills also transformed the style into a nationally appre-

his father, a fiddler, at house parties and barn dances. His first instrument was the mandolin, but over the years, Wills became a premier "breakdown" fiddler and it was as a player of that instrument that his reputation was made.

Restless throughout his life, Wills weathered four unsuccessful marriages and was prone to alcoholic binges. He spent many of his teenage years traveling through Texas as a hobo, working odd jobs. He would drift back to Turkey from time to time, but he left there for good following run-ins with the law and an arrest for rowdiness.

At this time, Wills was master of an enormous repertoire of folk and country tunes

ciated form of big band music, tinged unmistakably with the aura of the American West. By no means a country purist, Wills hired horn, reed, steel guitar, and drum players—unprecedented at the time—and constantly injected spicier musical elements, especially Dixieland jazz and blues, into his tunes.

The son of musical parents, James Robert Wills was born in the east Texas town of Kosse on March 6, 1905. When he was eight, his family moved to Turkey, a town in west Texas, where Wills began accompanying

from the shows he and his father had put on; additionally, his nomadic travels as a young man and a stint with a traveling medicine show had exposed Wills to black folk music and spirituals, Spanish music, and cowboy songs. He put all these influences to use starting in 1929, in Fort Worth, when he hooked up with guitarist Herman Arnspiger to found The Wills Fiddle Band. The pair did a regular radio show and were joined the following year by vocalist Milton Brown, guitarist Durwood Brown, and banjo player "Sleepy" Johnson.

Their radio sponsor at the time was the Aladdin Lamp Company, and the band obligingly changed its name to The Aladdin Laddies.

When the Burrus Mills Flour Company assumed sponsorship, the Wills outfit changed its name again, this time to the Light Crust Doughboys. Wills finally objected to sponsor control when the president of Burrus Mills, W. Lee Daniel, who was also their announcer on Fort Worth's KFJZ and their manager (he later became governor of Texas), forbade the Doughboys from playing anywhere except on the radio show. This proscription caused Milton Brown to quit in 1933 and form his own outfit, Milton Brown and his Brownies, the group, it is generally agreed, that actually invented western swing. Wills also quit at this time, and moved to Waco, where he assembled the outfit that would ultimately become the legendary Texas Playboys.

Success after leaving KFJZ did not come easily. The dispute with Daniel was bitter and the spurned businessman used his considerable influence throughout Texas to deny Wills' new band regular radio work. The outfit, which consisted of Duncan Brown from the Doughboys; Wills' brother, Johnny Lee, on banjo; guitarists (and brothers) Kermit and June Whalin; and Everett Stover on trumpet, was doing fine at live performances in Waco, but radio appearances were necessary if the band was to reach the larger audiences Wills hoped for. In a decision that set them unerringly on a course for national stardom, Wills and company accepted an offer in 1934 from KVOO, a radio station in Tulsa, Oklahoma. It was from that pulpit that the Playboys' musical message was broadcast far and wide.

Drawing on his own fondness for the swing bands of Benny Goodman (1909–1986), Tommy Dorsey (1905–1956), and Earl "Fatha" Hines (1905–1983), Wills combined staccato Tex-Mex accordion and waltz and polka tempos popular with German immigrants in Texas to concoct a lively, upbeat western swing music that electrified audiences everywhere.

The Texas Playboys hit it big with such songs as "Texas Playboy Rag," "Mexicali Rose," and "Take Me Back to Tulsa." But it was "San Antonio Rose" in 1938, and a rewritten "New San Antonio Rose" in 1940, that marked the peak of their popularity. "New San Antonio Rose" became the group's first gold record; the crooner Bing Crosby (1904–1977) had a pop hit with it several years later.

Wartime restrictions such as gasoline rationing put a crimp in the mobility of all big bands, and by the end of World War II, interest in them began to wane. Wills moved to California in 1943 and re-formed the Playboys as a smaller outfit that continued to do well with live appearances and record sales through the 1950s. But he never again reached the pinnacle of the success he had had during the late thirties.

Failing health, including several heart attacks, slowed Wills down considerably in the sixties. He was elected to the Country Music Hall of Fame in 1968 and received the Academy of Country Music's Pioneer Award the following year. Though not as popular as it once was, western swing is still written and recorded, mostly in Texas, by contemporary bands such as Asleep At The Wheel.

Bob Wills died on May 13, 1975, in Fort Worth of complications resulting from a stroke he had suffered two years earlier while participating in a recording session—a reunion of the Texas Playboys.

The Grand Ole Opry

The music presented at the Grand Ole Opry in the 1930s was far more traditional than that sanctioned by the radio titans in Chicago and the movie moguls in Hollywood. The WSM broadcast featured mostly string band music and novelty acts. George Hay was interested in maintaining authenticity in order to enhance the prestige of the Opry, and he did so by setting down strict rules and guidelines that performers violated at their own risk.

There was a significant shift in the personnel format in 1938, however, when mountain fiddler Roy Acuff took the Opry stage, filling in for a member who had been suspended by Hay. A hillbilly personified, Acuff had a backup band, but it was his powerful voice and aching delivery that electrified

Before the Grand Ole Opry was moved to more modern quarters in the Opryland USA complex, its home was the drafty Ryman Auditorium (opposite page and below) near "Music Row" in Nashville.

listeners. So persuasive was his performance on that February night that letters of praise poured in for weeks afterward. On the strength of the fan mail, Acuff was invited to became an Opry regular. He reigned as the Opry's shining star, and then as its nostalgia champ, for the remaining fifty-four years of his life, establishing businesses and precedents along the way that were essential to Nashville's transformation into "Music City USA."

Acuff's arrival ushered in a new era at the Grand Ole Opry. String bands and ensembles gave way to individual stars, mostly singers, whose bands were almost incidental. But in 1939, another flamboyant wailer hit the Opry with music that relied heavily on instrumental virtuosity. Kentuckian Bill Monroe had concocted an intricate, driving, up-tempo brand of country music that eventually came to be called bluegrass. Audiences loved it. Bill Monroe's lightning

Roy Acuff (1903–1992)

If he had not been dangerously susceptible to sunstrokes, Roy Claxton Acuff might have had a career in professional baseball instead of becoming a pioneer in the efforts to make country music an international industry.

Augmenting Acuff's impressive credentials as a showman is his legacy as a major force in the business of country music. He was also an unsuccessful Republican candidate for governor of heavily Democratic Tennessee, and for twenty years was a perennial on the USO circuit. Roy Acuff was elected in 1962 to the Country Music Hall of Fame—the first living performer to be so honored.

The son of a fiddle-playing Baptist minister in Maynardsville, Tennessee, the young Roy Acuff showed almost no interest in music, but this is not to say he was not expressive. He was a gregarious youngster who enjoyed acting in school plays. Out of high school, Acuff won a minor league pitching position with the New York Yankees. It was during his brief tenure with a Yankees farm team that Roy discovered the susceptibility to sunstrokes that would force him to give up baseball and nearly every other outdoor activity. While recuperating from sunstrokes, Acuff taught himself to play the fiddle by listening to some of his father's recordings.

Acuff was able to put his burgeoning talents as a fiddler and his stage experience to good use when, at age twenty-eight, he signed on with a neighbor's Traveling Medicine Show. As a member of "Doc" Hauer's troupe, Acuff helped hawk a patent medicine called Moc-a-Tan by entertaining impromptu audiences with songs and musical sketches. It is not clear what benefits Moc-a-Tan promised, but Acuff benefited in at least two ways: he learned how to charm even skeptical audiences and he more than likely developed his booming singing style trying to reach those pre-amplification audiences.

Later in 1932, Acuff formed the Tennessee Crackerjacks. He soon renamed them The Crazy Tennesseans, and was on his way to stardom. In 1936, after three years of playing local venues, American Records in Chicago offered The Crazy Tennesseans a chance to record a number of songs. One of these was the Carter Family's "The Wabash Cannonball," sung during the sessions not by Acuff but by Sam "Dynamite" Hatcher. It became a regional hit in 1938. (The 1947 recording of "Cannonball" on the compact disc that accompanies this book features Acuff's vocal. It became a much bigger hit than the earlier recording.)

Another song put to wax in that 1936 session was "The Great Speckled Bird," an enigmatic and mystical gospel song based on a quote from the Book of Jeremiah. Its quirky appeal, and a lucky break, soon brought Acuff to the stage of the Grand Ole Opry, a platform he did not relinquish until his death.

Acuff had already failed three auditions for the Opry when, in 1938, fiddler Arthur Smith was suspended by the management. Acuff and his group were summoned as a last-minute replacement, bickering right up until showtime about the best way to capitalize on their unexpected big break.

Despite the quarreling among the bandmembers and the studio audience's polite but muted response to the outfit's debut performance, Roy Acuff left the stage a star.

At the time, Acuff told reporters that he was not comfortable with his performance and felt that maybe he had blown his big chance. But over the next several days, thousands of letters praising Roy Acuff arrived from listeners, and the Opry promptly invited him to become a regular. Throughout his prolific run, Acuff's roots remained firmly planted in the mountain and folk music first popularized by the Original Carter Family, whose themes were steeped in spiritualism and

pathos. Although Acuff eventually changed the name of his backup band from the Crazy Tennesseans to the more dignified Smoky Mountain Boys, he reveled in the moniker "King of the Hillbillies." As his stature and popularity grew, "King of the Hillbillies" was changed to "King of Country Music."

It was an apt title in more than one way. Acuff and songwriter Fred Rose—through their Acuff-Rose Music—laid the cornerstone that eventually transformed Nashville from an informal gathering place for musicians into a booming center of musical commerce. Acuff-Rose became a multimillion-dollar business that published sheet music and songbooks; operated its own recording studio and record company, Hickory Records; and booked tours, represented talent, and operated an overseas office. It remains one of the world's foremost country music publishing companies.

Acuff is remembered as an honest, down-to-earth man whose onstage antics included balancing his fiddle on his nose and showing off his vast collection of hand-painted ties. In 1974, when the Grand Ole Opry relocated, Acuff amused millions when he tried to teach President Nixon to use a yo-yo during the opening ceremonies.

Roy Acuff was an archtraditionalist who strongly resisted the appearance on the Opry of nontraditional songs and instruments even though his own debut had ushered the Opry into the era of the solo performer and away from its roots as a showcase for string bands and other multimember outfits. Acuff was criticized for stifling the growth of country music by resisting the appearances of honky-tonk performers and other talents whose style was at odds with Acuff's ideal. Quite a few performers either were denied access to the Opry or quit because of Acuff's dislike of electrified and other nontraditional instruments.

Roy Acuff was honored on many occasions during his lifetime. In addition to his 1962 election to the Country Music Hall of Fame, in 1987 he received a Lifetime Achievement Award from the National Academy of Recording Arts and Sciences, the organization that presents the Grammy Awards. In a 1991 televised ceremony from the Kennedy Center in Washington, D.C., Acuff was honored for his contribution to the performing arts. That year he was also presented with the National Medal of Art.

Roy Acuff died of congestive heart failure at Baptist Hospital in Nashville, on November 23, 1992.

Bill Monroe (1911–)

The "Father of Bluegrass Music" was born on September 13, 1911, on a farm in western Kentucky near the town of Rosine. In his lifetime he would create and popularize a unique music forged from the folk and gospel songs of the Appalachian region in which he lived and from the jazz and blues music he had encountered while growing up. Bluegrass is a distinct school that is fervently pursued today, mostly by virtuoso pickers and singers who are up to the rigorous requirements laid down by its founder.

The youngest of nine children by several years, Monroe, a very serious child, had a solitary childhood. His father was a hardworking farmer, and his mother, who died when Bill was six, was an enthusiastic fiddle player. He acquired traits from each that would serve him well in the career he ultimately chose, but it was probably his uncle Pendleton Vandiver, a skilled and popular local musician, who sparked Monroe's genius.

Even before his father died, the sixteen-year-old Monroe had mastered the mandolin, guitar, and fiddle. He enjoyed the impromptu string bands that performed at square dances and other functions, showcasing the mountain and folk music of the region. Monroe credits his Uncle Pen, who was in big demand locally as an admired fiddler, with teaching him the importance of musical timing and more; in "Uncle Pen," a song of tribute he wrote later in life, Monroe sings, "When Uncle Pen played the fiddle, how it would ring, Lord you could hear it talk, you could hear it sing."

Monroe was also impressed with a black guitarist friend named Arnold Schultz who was well versed in country and blues music. It wasn't unusual for Monroe on mandolin, Schultz on guitar, and Uncle Pen on fiddle to provide the music at socials and dances in and around Rosine. Fascinated by Schultz's blues guitar work, Monroe gradually incorporated blues riffs into traditional Appalachian melodies, a combination that formed the foundation of what became bluegrass.

Shape-note singing is another bluegrass element, one that Monroe undoubtedly heard as a member of both the Baptist and Methodist choirs in Rosine. An unadorned gospel style, shape-note relies heavily on sharp, quick harmonies, usually sung at full volume. With a strong, clear tenor, Monroe almost always sang the lead vocals when he began performing professionally.

At the age of eighteen Monroe left Kentucky to join two of his brothers who had found work in an automobile plant in Indiana. In their off-hours, Bill, Charlie, and Birch Monroe would pick and sing. In 1934, Bill and Charlie decided to pursue music full-time.

For four years the pair appeared (mostly in North and South Carolina) as The Monroe Brothers, impressing radio and concert audiences with their musicianship, especially their blistering instrumental dexterity. The two men were never at ease with each other, however, and their bickering became more and more

Bill Monroe at the Rosine, Kentucky, gravesite of his uncle and mentor, Pendleton Vandiver.

Monroe and his Blue Grass Boys in concert.

frequent, sometimes erupting into fistfights. By 1938 each had gone his own way, Charlie to form another group and Bill to form an ensemble called The Blue Grass Boys. It was only a year later, in 1939, that the Grand Ole Opry extended an invitation to The Blue Grass Boys to hop aboard.

Their skill was undeniable, but Monroe's outfit had not quite perfected the bluegrass style during its first several years on the Opry. With the emergence of Roy Acuff as a leading light on the show, the Opry sound was gradually shifting from its traditional orientation as a showcase for string bands to a showcase for singers who also happened to have bands. Monroe fit the bill perfectly. Monroe set the pace with his strident mandolin, he sang most of the lead vocals, and his "high, lonesome" tenor soared so forcefully in choruses that it became the standard to match for the many thousands of bluegrass outfits that followed.

It wasn't until the mid-forties that Monroe began the stylistic changes that culminated in the sound recognizable today as bluegrass. His premise seemed always to be virtuosity. Of the many musicians who came and went as members of The Blue Grass Boys—Lester Flatt, Earl Scruggs, and Vassar Clements among them—all were superb

players. The addition of Earl Scruggs' banjo to the existing ensemble of mandolin, fiddle, guitar, and bass was an especially distinctive touch, and Monroe's decision to let his musicians strut their stuff in impressive solos was the final defining element. By the 1950s, so many bands were playing Monroe's style that The Blue Grass Boys were periodically eclipsed. (The identifying term "bluegrass music" may have been coined during this period by fans who besieged disc jockeys with requests for "that blue grass music.")

Elvis Presley (1935–1977), Bob Dylan (1941–), Ricky Skaggs (1954–), and George Jones are among the many luminaries who cite Bill Monroe as a prime influence on their careers. Unlike country or country-western music, bluegrass found and kept huge audiences in all parts of the United States. Even in New England, long allergic to music from Nashville, bluegrass flourishes in festivals and among players who never tire of working out such tunes as "Blue Moon of Kentucky," "Orange Blossom Special," "Muleskinner Blues," and "Kentucky Waltz."

Bill Monroe was elected to the Country Music Hall of Fame in 1970. In 1984, he was awarded a presidential citation for contributions to American culture.

Ernest Tubb, an early proponent of honky tonk, was an admirer of Jimmie Rodgers. Here, Tubb is holding a guitar that once belonged to the Blue Yodeler.

mandolin work, the obvious skill of his backup band, and the haunting, "high, lonesome" blues-tinged vocals of The Blue Grass Boys caught on quickly. It is a great tribute to Monroe that over the years bluegrass has remained one of the few forms of country music unaffected by the vagaries of popular taste or the dictates of country music's power brokers. Bluegrass is preserved and played today by musicians around the world in more or less the same form that was developed by Bill Monroe.

In the late thirties, a flotilla of new stars arrived in Nashville, riding the wake of Acuff and Monroe. Many wore cowboy hats and the fringed, brocaded western-style outfits of the Hollywood cowboys. Texas-born Ernest Tubb (1914–1984) was a Jimmie Rodgers admirer who pioneered the honky-tonk school of country music in the early forties. Tubb met and befriended Carrie Rodgers, the Blue Yodeler's widow, who introduced him to executives at Decca Records.

Tubb's breakthrough 1941 hit on Decca, "Walking the Floor Over You," proved that an earnest heart could overcome limited vocal skill and propel a determined and otherwise talented individual to stardom.

Tubb's legacy as a founder of honky tonk was established when he became the first major country performer to use an electric guitar. Soon after, he added a drum set to his musical arsenal, something that was unheard of at the time. As his fame grew, Tubb insisted on recording in Nashville, compelling Decca to open an office there, another important step in the development of that city as the capital of country music.

Tennessee crooner Eddy Arnold (1918–   ) gave country music an important push by expanding its appeal to huge new audiences. Although he was billed as "The Tennessee Plowboy," Arnold was neither a hillbilly nor a honky-tonk performer. His smooth ballads crossed over into pop music, and his willingness to incorporate noncountry elements into the songs he recorded brought Arnold his great success. It is also likely that Arnold's accessible style piqued the interest of many listeners who had not yet sampled country music, inspiring them to explore the work of more orthodox country performers.

Balladeer Eddy Arnold pleased millions with his smooth crooning. Not an authentic country singer, Arnold nevertheless reached vast new audiences with his smooth hybrid of the style.

Lester Flatt (1914–1979) and Earl Scruggs (1924–   )

Guitarist Lester Flatt and banjo player Earl Scruggs were early disciples of the bluegrass pioneer Bill Monroe; they were also members of his Blue Grass Boys until they broke away in a bitter 1948 split to form Flatt & Scruggs and the Foggy Mountain Boys. That band lasted a little over twenty years, but ended when a similarly serious rift erupted, causing Earl Scruggs to leave his longtime partner to form the Earl Scruggs Review.

Lester Raymond Flatt was born on June 19, 1914, to a sharecropper family in Overton County, Tennessee. As a boy and a young man he worked in textile mills in Sparta, Tennessee, and Covington, Virginia. His love of the blues and his talent as a singer and guitar player later led to stints with a number of musical groups, including the Harmonizers in 1939, and the Happy Go Lucky Boys in 1941. Flatt spent 1943 and 1944 as man-

dolin player and tenor vocalist with Charlie Monroe's Kentucky Pardners and was recruited by Charlie's more famous younger brother, Bill, to join The Blue Grass Boys in Nashville. By this time, Monroe had already established himself as a star of the Grand Ole Opry and was developing bluegrass.

A brand-new member of the Blue Grass Boys himself when Lester Flatt arrived, Earl Scruggs had electrified Grand Ole Opry audiences with his virtuosic three-finger picking style, which allowed him to let loose a flurry of syncopated notes at a furious rate. The banjo had traditionally been thought of as a comic instrument, used mostly by clowns and comedians because of its peculiar look and sound. But in the hands of Earl Scruggs, the instrument became a serious musical tool, and Bill Monroe, a serious man, often let Scruggs take lead parts.

Born on January 6, 1924, in Flint Hill, North Carolina, Earl Scruggs had a back-

Above: Lester Flatt (far left) and Earl Scruggs (far right) on tour with the Foggy Mountain Boys. The pair met as members of Bill Monroe's Blue Grass Boys and pursued a successful post-Monroe career with their own Foggy Mountain Boys. A feud over the new group's musical direction eventually resulted in a split between Flatt and Scruggs. Opposite: Lester Flatt (left) and Earl Scruggs.

ground similar to that of Lester Flatt. Unlike Flatt, however, Scruggs was a prodigy, who had learned to play banjo before he entered the first grade. He picked up a love of the blues as a child, and began plunking in the three-finger style familiar in his region of North Carolina. He was a member of several bands as a young man, including the Carolina Wildcats and the Morris Brothers, and he worked in textile mills in both North and South Carolina during World War II. Moving to Nashville in 1945, Scruggs played for a time on a WSM broadcast with "Lost" John Miller; when Miller quit the business, Scruggs was hired by Bill Monroe and moved up to the Grand Ole Opry.

Flatt and Scruggs stayed with Bill Monroe for three years. In 1948, Scruggs left The Blue Grass Boys to carve out a career of his own, and Flatt came along. Monroe was unhappy about their departure, and considered it a betrayal, a wound that was never healed.

Scruggs made his banjo the lead instrument and began writing "breakdowns" for the instrument that imitated the swift, staccato fiddle style that had been popular in folk music for generations. Flatt & Scruggs and the Foggy Mountain Boys signed a contract with Mercury Records and began selling music similar to what they had played with Bill Monroe. Their first instrumental release was "Foggy Mountain Breakdown," one of the most famous bluegrass compositions.

Touring almost constantly during the fifties, the band became one of the premier bluegrass outfits in the United States by 1960. The folk revival that was occurring at that time broadened their audience, and they entered popular culture as authors of "The Ballad of Jed Clampett," the theme song for the television show *The Beverly Hillbillies*. Not long afterward, Flatt & Scruggs and the Foggy Mountain Boys became the first bluegrass band to perform at New York City's prestigious Carnegie Hall.

Differences in philosophy led to a breakup in 1969. Earl Scruggs had begun tinkering with bluegrass, which had remained virtually unchanged since 1948, adapting songs written by folk-rock writers as well as songs written by his three rock-oriented sons. Lester Flatt did not approve, and The Foggy Mountain Boys disbanded.

Scruggs went on to form the Earl Scruggs Review, incorporating drums, electric guitars, piano, and even synthesizer. Flatt formed the Nashville Grass, a pure bluegrass ensemble that not surprisingly released several successful albums.

Lester Flatt died of heart failure on May 11, 1979, in Nashville. He was visited in the hospital by Earl Scruggs. The two hadn't spoken to one another in ten years. Telling a visitor about it, Flatt said, "It came as quite a surprise and made me feel real good. We had a lot of good memories together."

Arnold's first hit, "Each Minute Seems Like a Million Years" (1945), was followed by a quick succession of songs that set sales and longevity records. Among these were "I'll Hold You in My Heart," which in 1947 spent twenty-one consecutive weeks at the number one position, and "Bouquet of Roses" (1948), which remained on the Top 40 country singles charts for an astonishing fifty-four weeks.

Hank Williams (1923–1953)

During this period of exploration into the money-making potential of crossover acts, a young man named Hiram King Williams wandered onto the scene and, in a blazing but brief career that vividly demonstrated the impressive power of raw talent, produced the musical legacy that has earned him the reputation as the greatest country singer of all time.

Hank Williams was an unstable combination of passion, pain, and rural Southern magnetism who rampaged through his short life, fueled in his final years by alcohol, drugs, and a determination to die. His determination was re-warded on New Year's Day, 1953, in Oak Hill, West Virginia. After years of abuse, his heart simply quit. He was en route to a performance in Ohio, riding in the back seat of his car, which was being driven by a stranger. He had been drinking and taking pain-killers for days. He was twenty-nine years old.

The irony of Williams' lonely death is underscored by the shabby cir-cumstances. His fame at the time was international. His music could be heard nearly everywhere. If he had not quite yet become a legend in his own time, he was well on his way. What puzzled people most about Hank Williams' death was that it occurred just as he had achieved what he hoped for most in life—widespread acclaim for his musical talents.

Williams had worked virtually all his life. He worked his way out of near-poverty in Mount Olive, Alabama, where he was born on September 17, 1923. His father was a shell-shocked World War I veteran who was hospitalized when Hank was seven, never to rejoin the family. Williams worked to help his mother by selling newspapers and peanuts, shining shoes, and running errands.

Many consider Hank Williams the greatest country singer of all time. He was twenty-nine when he died of heart failure, brought on by years of drug and alcohol abuse.

By the time he was fourteen, Williams was a street musician, playing guitar as taught to him by a local street singer named Rufus Payne. Williams was writing songs by then, and he won a talent contest with a number called "WPA Blues." He formed a band called The Drifting Cowboys and began learning the rough lessons of the musical trade by playing regular dates in a number of Alabama honky-tonks that were so rough they were ominously called "blood buckets." At the age of seventeen, Williams moved to Texas, but when World War II broke out he returned to Alabama to work as a welder in the Mobile shipyards.

Determined to make it big in the music business, Williams headed for Nashville at the close of the war. He had already met Roy Acuff in Alabama when he played as the local opener for a Grand Ole Opry traveling show and had even sold a song to Opry star Pee Wee King, but Williams was still a primitive talent. Never-

Audrey, Lucretia, Hank Jr., and Hank Williams Sr. Williams' marriage to Audrey foundered because of his excessive lifestyle.

theless, on his arrival in Nashville in 1946 the bold twenty-three-year-old song-writer headed straight for the office of music publisher Fred Rose. After listening to six or seven songs, Rose offered Williams a publishing contract. It was the beginning of a mentor relationship that lasted until Williams' death.

As a protégé of one of Nashville's most powerful publishers, Williams was on his way to stardom, and Rose skillfully guided the young songwriter's career, landing him a deal with a local label called Sterling Records; this deal eventually led to a contract with nationally distributed MGM records. Rose also helped Williams get a regular position on a Shreveport radio show called *Louisiana Hayride*.

He soon became the headliner on *Hayride*, performing there for two years and occasionally issuing hit records like "Move It On Over," "I Heard You Crying in Your Sleep," and "Lovesick Blues," a Tin Pan Alley standard that sold extremely well. "Lovesick Blues" sold so well, in fact, that on the strength of its popularity, Williams was invited to perform at the Grand Ole Opry. His debut on June 11, 1949, was spectacular—the audience brought him back for six encores of "Lovesick Blues." Even though his alcohol abuse was well known, the Opry hired him as a regular.

Almost immediately after joining the Opry, Williams' career skyrocketed. Within a year he was country music's biggest star. He and The Drifting

Cowboys launched a series of grueling tours throughout the nation, into Canada, and even to Germany to entertain U.S. troops. And the hits kept coming: "Why Don't You Love Me?," "Cold, Cold Heart," and "Long Gone Lonesome Blues." Williams' records were bought even by people who didn't follow country music. His appeal was universal. People sensed the sincerity of his songs and responded to the unadorned straightforwardness of the emotions they expressed.

While his fame was building, Williams' personal life was collapsing. The Opry fired him for drunkenness in 1952. His wife Audrey, who had encouraged his foray to Nashville, divorced him. He returned to Shreveport to regroup on *Louisiana Hayride*, but ended up a laughingstock for his public marriage to a local beauty for which admission was charged.

The week before Williams died, his song "I'll Never Get Out of This World Alive" hit number one. His last performance, a benefit at the Elite Cafe for the American Federation of Musicians, took place on December 28, 1952, in Montgomery, Alabama. He died three days later in his Cadillac, probably while asleep, on the way to Canton, Ohio, for another show. (Williams' self-destructive lifestyle was the prototype for several country performers, including the talented Lefty Frizzell.)

Songs he had recorded before his death, "Your Cheatin' Heart," "Kawliga," and "I Won't Be Home No More," among them, were released and became hits. They entered the mainstream of American music with the same impact and resonance as his many other hit songs, a brief list of which includes "I Can't Help It (If I'm Still in Love with You)," "Hey Good Lookin'," "Jambalaya," "Settin' the Woods on Fire," and "I'm So Lonesome I Could Cry."

When the Country Music Hall of Fame opened, eight years after he died, Hank Williams was one of the first three people to be inducted. His mentor Fred Rose and Jimmie Rodgers were the other two.

Lefty Frizzell (1928–1975)

Lefty Frizzell, who was an innovative and very troubled man, is acknowledged by many of country music's major stars as a prime influence on their careers. His wrenching singing style, in which notes and syllables are tortured and stretched, is the foundation for much of the distinctive vocalizing in country music. Performers such as George Jones, Merle Haggard, Randy Travis, and Clint Black all acknowledge Frizzell as their vocal ideal.

Frizzell himself was a disciple of the "Blue Yodeler," Jimmie Rodgers, whose records left a vivid impression on him. Frizzell also cited honky-tonk pioneer Ernest Tubb as a major inspiration—and it was in the realm of honky tonk that Frizzell left his mark.

Born in Corsicana, Texas, on March 31, 1928, William Orville Frizzell was the son of an oil rigger who moved around a lot. A country music fan, his father encouraged the boy to take up the guitar and often sang along with the Jimmie Rodgers and Ernest Tubb tunes the boy learned to play. Frizzell's talent was such that he was able to find work as a solo entertainer even before he was a teenager; before he was old enough to legally drink alcohol, Frizzell was performing in bars and nightclubs, earning the nickname "Lefty" because of his effective left hook.

Nashville soon got wind of the charismatic young country singer, and Columbia Records released Lefty's "If You've Got the Money, I've Got the Time" in 1950. It was an immediate hit, rising to number one on the country chart. The flip side, "I Love You a Thousand Times," went to the top of the chart the following year. Frizzell was so popular with crowds during the early fifties that they sometimes mobbed him, and even tore his clothes—a preview of the mania that would surround Elvis Presley three or four years later. Frizzell had a string of hits in 1951: "I Want to Be With You Always," "Always Late," and "Mom and Dad's Waltz," but problems with alcohol, which hounded him throughout his life, led Frizzell into a period of artistic inactivity that did not end until he released "Long Black Veil" in 1959.

Frizzell's unreliability, which was mostly due to alcohol abuse, caused Columbia Records to drop him in 1972. ABC Records picked him up almost immediately, but Frizzell died of complications resulting from a stroke in 1975. His career had been checkered, but the songs he recorded and his unique singing style were a revelation to his peers and to many country musicians who followed. Lefty Frizzell was inducted into the Country Music Hall of Fame in 1982.

Chet Atkins has contributed to the development of country music as a musician, talent scout, record company executive, and co-architect of the "Nashville Sound."

The Nashville Sound

The postwar boom years were happy times in Nashville. With money in their pockets and a hankering to have some fun, Americans were buying records, going to concerts, and plunking change by the handful into jukeboxes. The business of country music was humming right along. The Grand Ole Opry reached ten million listeners every Saturday night on network radio, television exposure was becoming more and more frequent, and the music now had its own fan magazines, radio stations, and record and music publishing companies. But even before complacency could set in, things changed dramatically—rock and roll was born. Its popularity would send Nashville reeling. Young record buyers were all shook up by the new sound that was mostly the purview of white Southern boys heavily into African-American rhythms and the blues. As more and more rock records were issued, it became clear to radio programmers that rock was much more than a passing fad, and many country stations switched formats.

This had a dramatic effect in Nashville. The emergence of rock did not immediately affect the style or popularity of stalwarts such as Webb Pierce (1926–1991), George Jones, or Kitty Wells, but it did lead a number of other country performers to drop the fiddle and steel guitar and adopt the smoother pop sound that had worked so well for the likes of Eddy Arnold. Though some

George Jones (1931–   )

Very few country music lovers would dispute that George Jones is one of the greatest country singers of all time. They would not only be talking about his voice and the way he sings a song, wrenching from it every smattering of emotion and nuance in a way that lacks guile or obvious theatricality, but also about his life, which has been a caricature of the brawling, hard-drinking, down-and-out, dissolute hero of so many country songs. Jones' life and career have teetered on the razor edge of oblivion more than once. His indisputable talent as a singer has repeatedly saved his professional life from the ravages of his personal life. In his time, Jones has lived through drug and alcohol addiction, arrests on drug and alcohol charges, a charge of armed assault, a near-fatal car crash, bankruptcy, and the nickname "No Show Jones," a title conferred upon him by countless concert promoters. But he has persevered, remaining an artistic inspiration to an entire generation of country performers.

The son of an alcoholic truck driver and a Pentecostal Baptist church pianist, George Jones was born on September 12, 1931, in Saratoga, Texas. When George was very young, the family moved from town to town, and his father eventually took a steady job as a pipefitter at the shipyards in Beaumont, Texas. Evidently George was frequently physically abused, and by the time he was fourteen he had left home, supporting himself by playing backup guitar with a variety of small-time bands in Texas. By the time he was eighteen, he had married, and abandoned, his wife and first child. Following a three-year enlistment in the Marines, Jones met a producer for Houston's Starday label in 1955 and recorded "Why Baby Why" and "You Gotta Be My Baby," both of which became hits. These were released at the time Elvis Presley, Carl Perkins, and other rockabilly singers were burning up the charts with their exciting rock and roll music; Jones saw the commercial potential and recorded a string of rockabilly songs, which he hoped would prove as successful for him. He later came to regret this strategy, and as a successful country singer he even tried to find and buy back his earliest recordings, saying that he wasn't at all proud of them.

Despite his false start, Jones soon began singing in a powerful honky-tonk style, and he was invited to join the Grand Ole Opry. Hits such as "White Lightning" (1959) followed; with these hits, fame and troubles with alcohol and drugs began to plague him. Jones became infamous for missing concerts entirely, leaving them early, or arriving too late. He was sued many times by promoters who had lost money on what turned out to be phantom events. Still, the early 1960s saw Jones recording such hits as "She Thinks I Still Care" (1961), "We Must Have Been Out of Our Minds" (a 1963 duet with Melba Montgomery), and the very popular crossover hit "The Race is On" (1964).

In the mid- and late 1960s, Jones' tumultuous personal life stabilized briefly when he began touring and performing with Tammy Wynette, whom he married in 1968. The two were extremely popular with audiences, and they scored big hits with tunes such as "Take Me" (1972) and "Let's Build a World Together" (1973). But Jones ultimately reverted to self-destructive behavior and he and Wynette were divorced in 1975 (they nonetheless continued their professional association).

By 1979 the demands of creditors, mostly people suing him, had grown so great that Jones declared bankruptcy. He also checked into a hospital, hoping to dry out. This lull may have allowed him to collect himself enough to record the classic "He Stopped Loving Her Today" (1980), a spectacularly

In a career filled with precipitous ups and downs, George Jones has survived as one of country's most beloved and influential talents.

successful record and a performance that impressively showcased Jones' exceptional command of his craft. His personal demons had merely been beaten back, however, not exorcised. Another hospitalization in 1982 failed to prevent his 1983 arrest in Mississippi for cocaine possession and public drunkenness. Following his release from jail, he flipped his car, nearly killing himself in the wreck.

If 1983 was a low point in Jones' life, however, it was also the year that marked the beginning of his resurrection. He married Nancy Sepulveda, a woman he had met several years earlier at a concert in New York,

and he credits her with helping him conquer his addictions. Moreover, he made a conscious decision to retake control of his career, and prohibited producers such as Billy Sherrill from soaking his music in the Nashville Sound. Jones returned to his roots as a honky-tonk singer, releasing such superb albums as *My Very Special Guests* and *Shine On*.

Acknowledged by most of today's neotraditionalist country superstars as a major influence, George Jones continues to record today in the style that brought him his greatest fame and that has touched the hearts and minds of countless fans.

people would disagree, it was probably the invention of the "Nashville Sound" in the early fifties, by the skilled guitarist and record producer Chet Atkins (1924–   ) and his colleague, producer Owen Bradley, that saved country music from extinction.

Atkins worked as a talent scout and record producer for RCA in Nashville, and became a considerable star in his own right as a guitar player. Bradley ran Quonset Studios in town, produc-

Jim Reeves (top) was the most popular country singer of the late fifties and early sixties. His career ended tragically in a plane crash near Nashville in 1964. Ray Price (above) rose to international fame in the fifties as a hard-edged honky-tonk singer. In a deliberate career move, he switched to ballads in the sixties and remained spectacularly popular as a crooner.

ing such hits as Kitty Wells' "It Wasn't God Who Made Honky Tonk Angels." Both men recollect that their experiments with string sections, steel guitars, and the soupy background vocals that characterize the Nashville Sound were meant to add exciting new elements to country music and to differentiate it from rock. For a while, the overblown arrangements worked. The country-pop hybrid rejuvenated the careers of such singers as Jim Reeves (1924–1964), Ray Price (1926–   ), and Patsy Cline. It was also seized upon by newcomers like Marty Robbins, Sonny James (1929–   ), and Conway Twitty (1933–1993).

Kitty Wells (1919–)

Kitty Wells, the first female superstar in the notoriously male-dominated country-music business, would be the first to reject the title "feminist." She has told interviewers that "women are supposed to be the weaker sex, and men are supposed to take care of them," and she was thrilled when former Tennessee governor Frank Clement described her as "an outstanding wife and mother, in keeping with the finest traditions of Southern womanhood." Nonetheless, throughout her career as a solo performer and in appearances with her husband, Johnny Wright, Wells was the first performer to regularly bring a woman's point of view to country music.

With rare exceptions such as Patsy Montana, women in the early days of country music were familiar mostly as members of singing groups, or they appeared as featured "girl singers" to support male stars. When Kitty Wells began her career in 1936, she was a girl singer backing up her husband over Nashville radio station WSIX. Wells continued in that role when Wright teamed up in 1939 with singer Jack Anglin to form the popular act they called Johnny and Jack. As time went by, Kitty landed her own recording contracts and released a succession of hit records, often promoting them with solo appearances. Her presence onstage as a main draw was a significant step in clearing the way for the acceptance of future female country stars, from Patsy Cline to Loretta Lynn to k.d. lang.

Kitty Wells was born Muriel Deason in Nashville on August 30, 1919, into a staunchly traditional family. When she was seventeen, Muriel married Johnny Wright, who came up with a stage name for Muriel, taking the handle from the folk song "Sweet Kitty Wells."

Wells hit her stride between 1949 and 1960, starting with a string of "answer songs" that put a woman's slant on hit songs by male artists. Her debut, "It Wasn't God Who Made Honky Tonk Angels" (1952), was a response to Hank Thompson's "The Wild Side of Life," which opens with the line "I didn't know God made honky tonk angels" and goes on to describe the loose morals of women who hang out in honky tonks. In her song, Wells argues that men are also to blame if a woman strays. "Honky Tonk Angels" zoomed to the number one position on the *Billboard* Country Chart, which was created in 1944. Wells was the first woman ever to perch there. It was during that period that she and Johnny and Jack were invited to appear on the Grand Ole Opry.

After a few more successful answer songs, Wells began recording original songs. She built a sublime body of work, mostly tearjerkers, in her distinctive, low-key, and sparse honky-tonk style. Between 1952 and 1965, she racked up thirty-five top ten hits with such songs as "Release Me," "I Can't Stop Loving You," "Cheatin's a Sin," and "Makin' Believe." Her thick, pure-country style fell out of favor with radio stations in the sixties, though not before she issued two of her best-loved songs, "Heartbreak USA" and "Will Your Lawyer Talk to God."

Kitty Wells was inducted into the Country Music Hall of Fame in 1976; she was presented with a Lifetime Achievement Award in 1991 by the National Academy of Recording Arts and Sciences.

Patsy Cline (1932–1963)

Patsy Cline's tragically short run as a top recording artist came at a time when Nashville was struggling to halt, or at least slow, the encroachment of rock and roll, which was beginning to cut significantly into radio time and record sales. Cline reigned with Kitty Wells at the top of the charts during a period of fundamental change in Nashville. While Wells stuck with a more traditional approach to country music, which, unfairly or not, eventually cost her the allegiance of radio programmers (though she remained popular with concert crowds), Cline got aboard the new country-pop bandwagon, reluctantly at first, and was just beginning to reap its rewards when she died in a plane crash in 1963.

Virginia Patterson Hensley was born on September 8, 1932, in Gore, Virginia. She was a lively youngster who soon became adept at tap dancing and playing the piano. Virginia (or Patsy, as she soon came to be called) was encouraged to sing by her mother, and the two often performed duets in church. Virginia's early exposure to music may have been the main inspiration for her run at a singing career, and as a teenager she landed a number of singing jobs, including a stint with a small-time country band called Bill Peer and his Melody Boys.

She married Gerald Cline (about whom not much is known) in 1952 and divorced him five years later, but kept the name Cline professionally.

As a young woman, Cline made several treks to Nashville in efforts to advance her career. She even appeared on Roy Acuff's WSM *Dinner Bell* radio show, a broadcast that always featured conservative, traditional country talent. But Nashville was changing from a loose confederation of like-minded country artists and businessmen into a bottom line—oriented entertainment machine; performers like Cline who had grown up embracing the songs of country's pioneers were finding that record companies were less and less interested in recording that kind of material.

Mostly through perseverance, Cline landed a recording contract in 1955 with a shady California-based outfit called the 4 Star Sales Company. She was paid a single fee for each song she recorded and was prohibited from singing material other than songs provided for her by 4 Star. It was a dreary and not very productive association, probably because of the lackluster songs with which she was saddled. But she was making records, and even though they were mostly unspectacular, Cline had her chance to make a mark in the business.

Her fortunes changed when she began working with producer Owen Bradley, one of the architects of the Nashville Sound, which was then beginning to take shape. Bradley and colleagues like Chet Atkins were hoping to bolster the fast-fading popularity of hillbilly music by toning down its twangier elements in favor of the more marketable pop sound. Pasty Cline was a reluctant contributor to the hybrid, but nevertheless recorded the bouncy "Walking After Midnight" in November 1956, under Bradley's guidance.

It was her appearance on Arthur Godfrey's *Talent Scouts* television show several months later that alerted the nation to "Walking After Midnight." Her bluesy rendition that night thrilled the audience and they gave her a standing ovation. The record took off, jetting to the number three position on *Billboard's* country chart. It also rose to number seventeen on the pop charts.

Despite this success, Cline remained reluctant to break with her country roots. This was reflected in her stage show, which was traditional enough to win her an invitation in 1960 to join the Grand Ole Opry. But it wasn't until 1961, after the birth of a daughter conceived with her new husband, Charles

I Get Through With You (You'll Love Me Too)." The following year she made the Top Ten with "Sweet Dreams (Of You)," probably her most characteristic number.

"Sweet Dreams" was released posthumously. On March 3, 1963, as she was returning to Nashville from a benefit performance in Kansas City, Cline and three friends were killed when the plane in which they were flying crashed in bad weather near Camden, Tennessee. Cline was thirty-one years old. She had been performing for more than twenty of those years, but recording for less than eight. Her relatively small collection of songs was potent enough to sustain her popularity through the seventies, and more than a few of her recorded performances will always be thought of as country-music classics.

Patsy Cline's influence on country music was vast. She and Kitty Wells were the first women to rise to the top of their profession on merit, easing acceptance for such women as Loretta Lynn, Tammy Wynette, and Dolly Parton, all of whom were on the way up in the early sixties. Musically, much of the work done by Cline and Owen Bradley is as impressive and evocative today as it was more than thirty years ago. A recently released album of her greatest hits sold more than three million copies and was certified triple platinum in 1991. Cline's life was dramatized in the film *Sweet Dreams* (1985), starring Jessica Lange. She was honored by her colleagues in 1973 by being inducted into the Country Music Hall of Fame.

Dick, that Cline scored her next hit record—two hits in fact—the classic country weeper "I Fall To Pieces" and the pop hit "Crazy," written by Willie Nelson.

4 Star had by then shut down, one step ahead of the law, and Cline's new label was Decca Records. With a wealth of material suddenly available to her, hits followed hits. In 1962 there was "She's Got You" and "When

As the fifties turned into the tumultuous sixties, television continued to grow as a prime force in defining pop culture. It wasn't long before the singers of the new, more accessible Nashville Sound ended up on television, which became an important new medium for country music, bringing the biggest names in the field into homes where they otherwise would never have visited. Patsy Cline's appearance on Arthur Godfrey's *Talent Scouts* in 1957 was a big boost to her career, and other country artists had similar experiences on other shows. The appearance of *The Johnny Cash Show* on ABC was a clear indication of the inroads country music had made into the mainstream. CBS offered *Hee Haw*, starring Buck Owens (1929–), Roy Clark (1933–), and a host of big country talent. Even though *Hee Haw* was an irreverent farce along the lines of NBC's *Rowan & Martin's Laugh-In*, it lasted for two seasons on CBS, and continued to be produced in syndication until 1993. With the arrival of the seventies, artists such as Kenny Rogers and Glen Campbell used the mainstream

Buck Owens (standing, center) and the regular cast of television's Hee Haw, *a country music variety show that remained on the air for more than twenty years.*

Tammy Wynette (1942–   )

A beautician from Mississippi, Virginia Wynette Pugh earned her stardom through ambition, determination, and the help of Nashville producer Billy Sherrill. Her recorded material and her tumultuous personal life, which includes five marriages, numerous hospitalizations for depression, and a kidnapping, have brought her the moniker the "Heroine of Heartbreak."

Wynette was born on May 15, 1942, on her grandfather's cotton farm in Itawamba County, Mississippi, and was reared by her grandparents. Her father, a cotton farmer and guitarist, died when Virginia was eight months old, and her mother traveled to Birmingham, Alabama, to work in a defense plant—not uncommon work for women in the war years.

Married for the first time at seventeen, divorced at twenty, Wynette worked as a hairdresser in Birmingham to support her three children, one of whom had spinal meningitis. Even as a girl Wynette had dreamed of a career as a country performer; as a young woman she made several pilgrimages to Nashville, none of which paid off until she met Billy Sherrill, who saw her potential and agreed to help try to launch her career.

One of the first things Sherrill suggested was that Virginia Pugh change her name to Tammy Wynette, a much more likely handle for a country star. More importantly, he provided Wynette with top-notch musical material, including her first hit, "Apartment Number 9," and the follow-up, "Your Good Girl's Gonna Go Bad," one of 1967's biggest sellers. The next year Wynette released "D-I-V-O-R-C-E" and "Stand By Your Man," the records that have proved to be her high-water mark as a recording artist. In 1968 Wynette also married George Jones, one of country's biggest stars and a man with personal demons of his own. Their marriage, which was rocky from the start, ended in 1975, though the pair continued to perform together and remained in demand at concerts for many years afterward.

The course of Tammy Wynette's career is something of a mystery to most people. The tabloid press has made much of her frequent hospitalizations and shock treatments for depression. The ransacking of her Nashville home and a reported kidnap attempt were widely seen as a bid for publicity when her career was at a low ebb. Despite all this, Wynette still has countless loyal fans.

Bob Dylan's decision to record his album
Nashville Skyline *in Music City USA gave country music a considerable boost in the minds of folk and folk-rock aficionados.*

awareness of country music to launch tremendously successful pop careers, using heavy doses of television to spread the word.

By 1970 the Nashville Sound had splintered into a myriad of different styles, each venturing further and further from the roots of country music. A "folk revival" in the sixties had little impact on Nashville, although Bob Dylan's decision to record *Blonde on Blonde* (1966) and *Nashville Skyline* (1969) there had a big influence on the eventual emergence of country rock.

The early efforts of Chet Atkins and Owen Bradley may have added a distinctive patina to mainstream country, but their sound was not appropriate for every artist and would later be criticized for nearly killing country music in a kind of "death by schmaltz." Nashville's zeal to rejuvenate sagging interest through strict control over musical content and the radical dilution of the original music by zealous commercializers eventually succeeded in alienating more than a few promising new talents. Instead of taking on the establishment on its home turf, these new voices set up shop elsewhere, most notably in Austin, Texas.

In Austin, both budding and established musicians found an atmosphere that wasn't charged with the hits-above-all-else mentality of Nashville. Musicians were free to cultivate a progressive, eclectic sound that often honored the past but also encouraged enlightened, intelligent experimentation. It was no paradise however; money was scarce, and without the commercial channels

Marty Robbins (1925–1982)

M arty Robbins was an eager purveyor of country pop, which swept Nashville in the late fifties and sixties. His work included cowboy ballads ("El Paso" and many other gunfighter songs), teen pop ("A White Sport Coat and a Pink Carnation"), and romantic, middle-of-the-road tunes ("My Woman, My Woman, My Wife"). He appeared in many movies, including *Ballad of a Gunfighter* (1963), and was one of the first country stars to perform in Las Vegas. He was also a skilled stock car driver and competed in the biggest NASCAR events.

Born on September 26, 1925, in Glendale, Arizona, Robbins was the grandson of a barker with a traveling medicine show who performed and collected cowboy songs. Enthralled by silver screen heroes like Gene Autry, Robbins recalled later that he would work all week picking cotton just to earn the price of admission to a Gene Autry movie.

Robbins joined the Navy at the age of nineteen, and began playing guitar and writing songs during his three-year tour, while he was stationed mostly in the Pacific. When he returned to Arizona, he began sitting in with a local country band, working by day as a ditch-digger in Phoenix. He eventually formed his own band, which became popular enough to win him a radio show and a weekly Phoenix television show called *Western Caravan*. One of the guests on the radio show was singer "Little Jimmie" Dickens, who was later instrumental in helping Robbins land a recording contract with Columbia Records in Nashville. His first release, "I'll Go On Alone" (1953), topped the country charts for two weeks.

Robbins' smooth style and his promise as a hit maker won him a spot on the Grand Ole Opry in 1953. His "Singing the Blues" (1956) topped the charts, though for the remainder of the fifties he recorded mostly teen-oriented pop songs, switching in the sixties and seventies to the pop ballads that made him famous.

A stock car enthusiast, Robbins was usually ranked among the top ten drivers on the NASCAR circuit, surviving a number of accidents along the way, including a spectacular 150-mile-per-hour crash in 1972 at the Daytona 500. Robbins gave up stock car driving, evidently not wanting to push his luck.

Chronic heart problems led to Robbins' death in Nashville on December 8, 1982. His musical legacy includes nearly seventy albums, eighteen number one pop and country hits (twelve of which he wrote), and two Grammy Awards for Best Country Vocal, Male.

Willie Nelson (1933–)

Willie Nelson's career has taken many bizarre and sometimes dangerous twists, but "The Redheaded Stranger" has survived them all to emerge as an immensely popular icon in American entertainment. His achievements in songwriting are considerable, his appeal as a recording artist and performer is legendary, and his appearances in movies and on television are as convincing and amiable as his beloved down-home personality.

As a boy in his hometown of Abbott, Texas, Willie Nelson would tune in to the Grand Ole Opry to hear the hillbilly music of Roy Acuff, the driving bluegrass of Bill Monroe, and the satisfying picking and singing of the many other Opry stars. In the cotton fields near his home he would listen to the cotton pickers singing "call back" blues; a line sung in one part of the field was answered by a picker in another part, and the exchange would continue, evolving into an impromptu song. Nelson's earliest desire was to become a musician.

His first experiences with music-making occurred while he still lived in Abbott, where he played guitar in a polka band and also in a western swing band. But the obstacles to an authentic career in music seemed insurmountable in his tiny Texas outpost.

Nelson then joined the Air Force, only to be discharged with a back injury. He returned to Texas and married a waitress named Martha Matthews, with whom he soon had three children. He worked many daytime jobs to support the family, including selling Bibles door to door and performing in bars and clubs at night. Nelson was also writing songs. In 1959 he sold the rights to a tune called "Family Bible" for fifty dollars. It became a Top Ten hit the following year for singer Claude Gray. He also sold the rights to "Night Life" for 150 dollars, and this has since become a country classic, been recorded by more than seventy artists, and appeared on nearly thirty million records over the years. Because he had transferred all rights, Nelson didn't see another dime from either of these compositions, but with the 150 dollars he had been paid for "Night Life," he bought a car and moved his family to Nashville.

His reputation as a marketable songwriter had already been established and Nelson continued to pen such hits as "Crazy" for Patsy Cline, "Hello Walls" for Faron Young, and "Funny How Time Slips Away," which has been recorded by more than eighty artists. But Nelson wanted to become a recording artist himself. While he managed to record two albums, and had a minor hit, a duet with his second wife called "Willingly," Nelson was consistently told by record company executives that his performance style wasn't nearly commercial enough and his voice was simply too odd. He continued to work as a musician, playing bass for several years in Ray Price's band. (Price was one of the Nashville stars who had had a major hit with Nelson's "Night Life.")

A near-tragedy in 1969 again changed the course of Nelson's life. A fire burned his home in Nashville, and he decided the time was right to head back to Texas, as Austin had become a musical refuge for Nashville's dispossessed. It was there that he teamed up with Kris Kristofferson, Waylon Jennings, Leon Russell, and other musicians and cultivated the antiestablishment brand of country music that came to be called outlaw.

The transformation worked. Nelson's 1971 album *Shotgun Willie*, and the subsequent releases *Phases and Stages* and *Red Headed Stranger* found a huge audience of country music lovers who had become bored with the pop leanings of Nashville. Nelson also tapped into a new, urban audience of countercultural types who were intrigued by

the bandanna-wearing maverick from Texas and his rough-riding cohorts. The 1976 release of *Wanted: The Outlaws* was such a spectacular sales success that even the Nashville establishment showered the twangy-voiced, smiling renegade with nearly every honor on the shelf.

Nelson's run as an outlaw was brief. He began recording songs in a number of styles and genres, including "Somewhere Over the Rainbow," "Georgia on My Mind," and "Blues Eyes Crying in the Rain," winning vast new audiences with the warm appeal of his voice, the very instrument the Nashville sages had warned would sink him.

In 1979 Nelson began a movie career, appearing in *The Electric Horseman* with Robert Redford. Subsequent films included *Honeysuckle Rose* (1980), *Thief* (1981), *Barbarosa* (1982), and *Red Headed Stranger* (1986). During this time, he also continued to put out hit songs, including "Mamas, Don't Let Your Babies Grow up To Be Cowboys," "On the Road Again," and "You Were Always On My Mind."

Willie Nelson has been instrumental in several high-profile causes, including the Farm Aid concerts, which were organized to help the economically pressed owners of small farms to survive. In an unprecedented "self-help" campaign, and to the amusement of his millions of fans, who probably appreciated the gesture's outlaw flavor, Nelson not long ago released an album to raise money to help pay the millions of dollars he owed the IRS in back taxes.

A unique figure in music who has defied every convention, Willie Nelson has managed to win and satisfy listeners in unthinkably broad categories with his warm and appealing voice and his obvious love for and dedication to his craft.

into which the new music could be funneled, Austin was a tough place to make a living. The appeal of the city was its reputation as a sanctuary from the formulaic music of Nashville, and the Texas capitol soon became a magnet for individuals and groups who worked up the rockabilly and eventually the progressive country music styles that are familiar today in the work of such artists as Joe Ely, Townes van Zandt, and Lyle Lovett. In 1975, public television station KLRU launched *Austin City Limits*, a showcase for the intriguing talents at work there. The broadcast was soon picked up by PBS, which airs it coast-to-coast today. But *Austin City Limits* and Austin itself now have quite a different cant than they had in those simpler days. The PBS broadcast is careful not to appear entirely mainstream, but make no mistake, the number of Nashville "establishment" acts it now features far outnumbers the lesser-known talents. And many musicians today consider Austin itself a training ground for Nashville; many hope to pay their dues in Texas in order to win their pensions in Music City USA.

Country singer-songwriter Lyle Lovett is equally comfortable playing blues, jazz, or folk music. His nomadic career, still relatively new, began in Texas, with stints in Dallas, Houston, and Austin. Lovett did some recording in Arizona before his career took off with a push from Nashville.

Merle Haggard (1937–   )

Merle Haggard's enormous body of work is an impressive example of musical integrity, and his unwillingness to bend to the demands of commercialization has won the allegiance of millions of fans and the admiration of his peers.

Born on April 6, 1937, in California, Haggard is the offspring of Depression era "Okies" who blew West after quitting their farms in the Dust Bowl and settled in Oildale, near Bakersfield. His young life was troubled and included stints in juvenile homes and in the California State Prison at San Quentin (for burglary). He was in solitary confinement in San Quentin on his twenty-first birthday, an experience that was evidently painful enough to put an end to his youthful run of delinquency. He recalled later that "I'm one guy...the prison system straightened out."

After he was released, Haggard returned to Bakersfield. In the early 1960s that city was called Nashville West because of its influential music scene that reveled in honky tonk and hard-edged country. Haggard began appearing as a backup guitar player at recording sessions and in bars in Bakersfield and Las Vegas. His association in 1962 with an enthusiastic Arkansan named Fuzzy Owen ultimately led to stardom.

Owen became Haggard's mentor and manager. In Owen's small studio Haggard recorded "Sing Me a Sad Song" and "All My Friends Are Gonna Be Strangers," both of which became hits. Their success led to offers from a number of big record companies and Haggard signed with Capitol Records on the condition that he be allowed to continue his collaboration with Fuzzy Owen.

Haggard's success was meteoric: nearly every one of the songs he recorded for Capitol rose high on the charts, among them "I'm a Lonesome Fugitive" and "Today I Started Loving You Again." By 1968 he was one of country music's top stars and he had a fearsome blue-collar following, to whom he endeared himself completely with "Okie From Muskogee" and the follow-up "The Fighting Side of Me."

Haggard was tagged as a spokesman for the nation's right wing, a role he never sought and did not want. Expectations that he would follow the two "fighting" songs with similarly patriotic numbers were frustrated when he instead returned to his main themes—the working man, the dashed lover, and the unfortunate prisoner.

Merle Haggard's music is an important bridge between the roots of country music and the contemporary hybrids of country and rock. His unique expressiveness is personal, not commercially stylized. Listeners respond as much to his powerfully evocative singing as they do to his truthful lyrics. With his band, The Strangers, Merle Haggard continues to pump out his distinctive combination of swing, blues, and jazz that draws unerringly from the deep well of country's roots.

The Outlaws

Despite its recent absorption into the mainstream musical scene, Austin in the seventies was a temporary hideout for several influential Nashville expatriates, among them Willie Nelson, Leon Russell, Kris Kristofferson, and Waylon Jennings (1937–   ), who came to be known as "the outlaws" because of their contempt for the Nashville establishment.

The chief outlaw would have to be Jennings, a gruff Texan who was touring with Buddy Holly's band when Holly was killed. Jennings escaped death in the February 3, 1959, plane crash that killed Holly and everyone else aboard by giving up his seat to J.P. Richardson ("The Big Bopper"). This close call and the loss of his friend Holly caused Jennings to leave the music-making business for several years, taking a job in Phoenix as a disc jockey. By the early sixties he had formed his own band called Waylon Jennings and the Waylors who had a

repertoire that consisted mostly of rock and country with a no-nonsense rock edge. The Waylors became well known in the Southwest, and as their reputation spread, talent scouts from both Nashville and Los Angeles came to see the group in Arizona.

It was Chet Atkins who convinced Jennings to sign with RCA Records in 1965, and Jennings soon moved to Nashville, where he and Johnny Cash became roommates. Cash was already a big star. His 1955 hit "Cry, Cry, Cry" and his subsequent hits "Folsom Prison Blues" (1956), "I Walk the Line" (1956), and "Ring of Fire" (1963) had brought him membership in the Grand Ole Opry and had made his name a household word. But in the mid-sixties, Cash's career was in a slump, and he and Jennings became infamous

Left to right: Willie Nelson, Waylon Jennings, Johnny Cash, and Kris Kristofferson, four of country music's "bad boys," in a concert to promote their album Highwayman II.

Kris Kristofferson (1936–   )

Kristofferson's career as an actor has obscured his impressive accomplishments as a songwriter and singer, mostly of country songs. His lonesome, tragic screen persona echoes the timbre of his musical catalog, which includes such mournful ballads of the dispossessed as "Me and Bobby McGee," "Sunday Mornin' Comin' Down," "Silver Tongued Devil and I," and "Why Me Lord?" His image as a scruffy, doleful, melancholy sort is also in sharp contrast to his early life as a Rhodes Scholar, an Army helicopter pilot, and a would-be instructor at West Point. The Brownsville, Texas, native has proven himself to be a jack of many trades and master of most of them, but his well-publicized problems with drugs and alcohol also show that the journey so far has not been smooth.

Kristoffer Kristofferson was born on June 22, 1936, into a military family (his father was an Air Force general). He was a model son, a Golden Gloves boxer, and a Phi Beta Kappa. He won the *Atlantic Monthly*'s collegiate short story contest and went to Oxford University on a Rhodes Scholarship. Returning to the United States in 1960, Kristofferson joined the Army, training and qualifying as a helicopter pilot; he also took up the guitar. When his tour ended, he reenlisted for a second three-year hitch and was sent to Germany, where other soldiers encouraged him to send some of his songs to Nashville. At the end of his second tour, Kristofferson returned to the States and contemplated a career at West Point.

Compulsively, and to the amazement and disapproval of his family, he instead moved to Nashville, arriving there with little more than the handful of songs he had written in Germany. The years that followed might just as well be taken from the story of any ambitious, would-be songwriter's biography; Kristofferson tended bar and even worked as a janitor at a Columbia Records studio as he tried to interest the reigning recording stars of the time in his material.

Roger Miller and Johnny Cash eventually responded to Kristofferson's persistence. Miller recorded "Me and Bobby McGee" and Cash made a number one hit of "Sunday Mornin' Comin' Down," which in 1970 was voted the Country Music Association's Song of the Year.

Cash and Kristofferson became friends, and with the star's encouragement, Kristofferson signed a recording deal with the Monument label, making albums that were firmly rooted in folk and country music. In spite of chronic stagefright, his tours were well received and "Silver Tongued Devil" and "Why Me Lord?" went gold. At about the same time, Janis Joplin transformed "Me and Bobby McGee" into a rock classic and a blockbuster sales champ.

In the early seventies Kristofferson went to Hollywood and began a film career, appearing in such movies as *Cisco Pike* (1971), *Alice Doesn't Live Here Anymore* (1975), *A Star Is Born* (1976), *The Sailor Who Fell From Grace with the Sea* (1976), *Semi-Tough* (1977), and *Heaven's Gate* (1980).

His marriage in 1973 to singer Rita Coolidge lasted only a few years, a period in which they toured the country as a country-pop duo and during which Kristofferson's drug and alcohol abuses worsened. His friendship and professional work with Willie Nelson and Waylon Jennings, themselves substance abusers,

earned him recognition as one of country music's outlaws, and in 1976, Kristofferson appeared on the highly successful album *Wanted: The Outlaws*.

His life in the years following his divorce from Coolidge was difficult, but Kristofferson managed to kick his addictions. He gravitated back to country music and discovered that Cash, Nelson, and Jennings were also drying out. He joined them on a 1990 tour to promote the album *Highwayman II*.

Now married to attorney Lisa Meyers, Kristofferson continues to write and act; his 1987 solo album, *Repossessed*, was widely praised, as were his performances in the movies *Amerika* and *Trouble In Mind*. Kristofferson retains his hard-won reputation as a sensitive chronicler of the vagaries of lost love, loneliness, and despair, crafting his songs with the sophistication of a would-be novelist and taking life, as he told one interviewer, "one day at a time."

Kris Kristofferson and his wife (at the time), Rita Coolidge, in concert.

Johnny Cash (1932–   )

Johnny Cash has performed many times inside prison walls. His early career was boosted by a live recording of a concert at Folsom Prison. Here, Cash performs at the California State Prison at San Quentin.

Probably the best-known country performer in America today, Johnny Cash has had a long, diverse, and eventful career. As a musical performer he has sung country, gospel, folk, and the blues; he has performed and recorded with talents as diverse as Carl Perkins, Jerry Lee Lewis, Roy Orbison, Bob Dylan, Merle Haggard, Waylon Jennings, Tom Petty, and George Harrison. He married June Carter, a daughter of the Original Carter Family's Maybelle Carter. He has acted in feature films and television movies, and he has written soundtracks for a number of films. Cash is rightly considered both a pioneer and a great contemporary innovator of country music.

Born on February 26, 1932, in Kingsland, Arkansas, Cash was the fourth of Ray and Carrie Cash's seven children. When Johnny was three, the family moved to Dyess, Arkansas, where they eventually bought and operated a cotton farm. The Cashes were charismatic Christians; relatives on both sides were Baptist preachers or missionaries, and there was a tradition of gospel singing in the household. There was also a fondness for traditional songs, and for the interpretation of those songs by the Original Carter Family, whose records and performances the Cashes heard on the radio.

Cash evidently decided early that he was not meant to farm cotton; he left Dyess soon after graduating high school and worked briefly in an Arkansas oleomargarine factory and an automobile plant in Pontiac, Michigan. He joined the Air Force in 1950 and served four years in Germany, where he began playing the guitar and transforming poetry he had written into songs, and later, composing songs outright.

After he was discharged in 1954, Cash settled in Memphis and married a woman named Vivian Liberto (they were divorced in 1966). He sold electrical appliances door to door and also formed a small gospel group with two friends, calling it Johnny Cash and the Tennessee Two. Their music-making was informal until Cash worked up the courage in 1955 to approach Memphis record producer Sam Phillips for help. On his Sun Records label, Phillips had recently introduced the world to such rockabilly acts as Elvis Presley, Jerry

Lee Lewis, Carl Perkins, and Roy Orbison. Phillips' advice to Cash was: drop gospel, think commercial.

Cash took this advice to heart, returning several months later with new material that impressed Phillips enough for him to offer the young man a contract. The single "Cry, Cry, Cry" on Sun Records was a regional hit in 1955, and was followed the next year by "Folsom Prison Blues" (released again in 1968) and "I Walk the Line." Johnny Cash was on his way to superstardom.

The Grand Ole Opry invited Cash to become a member in 1956, and he gladly moved to Nashville, where he spent the next two years writing, recording, and performing on WSM's most famous broadcast. Then, in 1958, Cash resigned from his regular Opry appearances in favor of hitting the road with his own traveling show, accepting frequent requests to make television appearances. Professionally, this decision paid off. Cash's road show toured the country through the 1960s, causing a great deal of excitement wherever it went. His television appearances eventually led to his own weekly network show on ABC from 1969 to 1971. By then Cash had mostly conquered his serious drug addiction, which had begun in the early sixties, when he frequently took amphetamines and barbiturates to make life on the road easier. His carousing in Nashville with contemporaries Waylon Jennings and Willie Nelson is the stuff of legend.

Surprisingly, drugs did very little outward damage to Cash's career. During the sixties, he began expanding his repertoire, writing and performing folk- and blues-based music and "plight" songs (songs about Native Americans and prison inmates, for example). He recorded regularly and brilliantly, and he kept his road show intact and functioning smoothly. His 1968 appearance at Folsom Prison in California, and the subsequent release of "Folsom Prison Blues" recorded there live, took him to number one on the charts.

In 1968 Cash also married June Carter, who, with her mother and sisters, had been a fixture in the road show, and whom Cash credits with being instrumental in helping him overcome his addictions.

Cash has appeared in feature films and made-for-television movies, among them *A Gunfight* (1970), *Pride of Jesse Hallam* (1981), and *Stagecoach* (1986). He has written soundtrack music for *The True West*, *Little Fauss and Big Halsy*, and *Pride of Jesse Hallam*. He was the producer and cowriter of *The Gospel Road* (1973) and he has written an autobiography, *The Man in Black*, and a novel, *The Man in White*, about the conversion of the Apostle Paul.

His discography is vast; the best estimates peg his record sales to date at fifty million. He has had more than 130 songs on the country chart, and nearly fifty on the pop chart. Johnny Cash was elected to the Country Music Hall of Fame in 1980. Despite heart bypass surgery in 1989, Cash continues to perform regularly today.

A well-groomed Waylon Jennings in the days before he became known as one of country music's "outlaws" and took on a scruffier appearance.

for their rowdiness and their rampant substance abuse. Both men later admitted publicly to serious problems with drugs and alcohol, which they both overcame, but during the late sixties neither seemed to think their addictions were much of a problem at all.

Cultivating a reputation in Nashville as a maverick, Jennings earned his keep with hit albums such as *Love of the Common People* and *The One and Only Waylon Jennings* (both 1967). To nearly everyone's astonishment he hired a New York–based manager, Neil Reshen, to help him win more artistic control over his work. Jennings seemed gleeful about flaunting his independence and gradually even began to look the part of an outlaw, adopting a long-haired, scruffy, leather-vested look that was in sharp contrast to the gaudy but well-groomed appearance of his early days. Jennings toured almost constantly and won legions of fans in nearly every part of the country with his straight-from-the-hip, thoroughly believable, soul-shaking music.

Eventually, Jennings hooked up with Willie Nelson, Kris Kristofferson, and other like-minded musicians who by this time were even calling themselves outlaws. Writing, recording, and touring without much regard for what the movers and shakers in Nashville thought became a way of life. For Jennings and Nelson as performers, it was an immensely successful way of life. Their 1976 release, *Wanted: The Outlaws*, on which Jennings' fourth wife, Jessi Colter, along with Kristofferson, Tompall Glaser, and Jack Clement, also appeared, was the first country album to be certified platinum (meaning that it sold more than one million copies). In his career, Jennings has won numerous Grammys and other awards; by the 1990s he had accumulated sixteen number one singles, nine gold records, two platinum albums, two double-platinum albums, and a quadruple-platinum album.

The incontestable economic and artistic success of the outlaws was still not enough to bust the Nashville bureaucracy. "The business" continued to bury

Charlie Daniels (1937–   )

Charlie Daniels has been a member of various no-name bar bands and has put in time as a songwriter and session player in Nashville, but his main pursuit and claim to fame has been as leader of the fiery and iconoclastic Charlie Daniels Band, whose bluegrass-to-boogie repertoire has been a favorite of arena concert crowds for more than twenty years.

Daniels was born in 1937 in Wilmington, North Carolina. Unlike many children who go on to careers in music, Daniels had no personal experience with singing or playing until he bought a guitar at the age of fifteen and taught himself to play by listening to Elvis Presley tunes and to WLAC, a black radio station. At seventeen, Daniels became enthralled by the bluegrass music of Bill Monroe. He was inspired to take up the fiddle and decided to make music his career.

Daniels paid his dues in a band called the Jaguars, performing mostly in bars and honky tonks throughout the South. A chance meeting with Nashville producer Bob Johnston in Fort Worth, Texas, got one of Daniels' tunes, "It Hurts Me," onto the flip side of an Elvis Presley record. It also led to Daniels' first album, produced by Johnston, which was a flop. Undaunted and convinced that Daniels had star potential, Johnston used his clout in Nashville to arrange some session work for the burly fiddler and guitarist.

Never an enthusiastic session player, Daniels nevertheless plugged away between 1966 and 1971, contributing to a number of groundbreaking albums, including Bob Dylan's *Nashville Skyline*. He was useful in Nashville for his command of many styles, from jazz to rock to bluegrass, but Daniels recollects that he was not very happy about playing "the usual Nashville thing." In 1971 he quit working as a session player and almost immediately formed the Charlie Daniels Band, hitting the road for what would become a regular touring schedule of as many as 250 shows a year.

Daniels' songs are mostly simple anthems centering on pride and can-do determination. Songs such as "In America" and "The South's Gonna Do It" honor the strength and nobility of working-class America. If his lyrics are light, however, his sentiments concerning patriotism and the American people are rock solid—and his musical accomplishments are impressively complex. It's not unusual in the course of a Charlie Daniels Band concert to be swept through a full range of contemporary styles—from pure country and rollicking bluegrass to full-bore, hard-driving rock.

Awarded a Grammy in 1980 for "The Devil Went Down to Georgia," Charlie Daniels is the host of the Volunteer Jam, an annual concert event that turns Nashville on its ear each summer.

its roots deeper and deeper under layers of artificial turf. The mainstream offerings in the mid- and late seventies were from singers such as Moe Bandy and Gene Watson who issued what amounted to parodies of what country music had become—songs with titles like "Her Body Couldn't Keep You Off My Mind" and "Honkytonk Amnesia."

Nashville's amnesia and its mania for crossover pop hits was critically diluting country music. In the eighties, slick, glittery performers such as Crystal Gayle, Olivia Newton-John, and Kenny Rogers reigned. Barbara Mandrell and Lee Greenwood were singing country-pop in Las Vegas. Hollywood produced *Coal Miner's Daughter*, an inspiring look at the life of Loretta Lynn, and *Urban Cowboy*, a movie that sent hundreds of thousands of country wannabes flying off mechanical bulls that were dutifully installed in bars around the country.

The Hats

Almost overlooked in the mediocrity of the eighties were separate debuts by two young men who would set the stage for a wholesale return to country music's roots and, along with it, an astounding resurrection of Nashville's fortunes. George Strait wandered up from the south Texas brush community of Pearsall and released an album called *Strait Country* in 1981. At about the

Ricky Skaggs is a virtuoso string performer and singer whose appearance on the country music scene in the early eighties helped rejuvenate a sagging industry.

same time, a Kentucky singer and guitar and fiddle genius named Ricky Skaggs was making his Nashville debut with an album called *Waitin' for the Sun to Shine*. Both records were heavy and eloquent doses of the kind of music that had made Nashville famous in the first place. Strait's influences were the west-

One of the so-called "hat acts," country singer Clint Black is among country's most popular figures, rocketing to fame by returning to the music's roots.

ern swing of Bob Wills and the confident vocal purity of George Jones; Skaggs was a bluegrass disciple of Bill Monroe and at least his equal in skill. Their debuts sold unexpectedly well, as did their subsequent albums. Strait's 1987 album, *Ocean Front Property*, was the first disc ever to debut at number one on the Billboard country chart.

The appearance of North Carolina's Randy Travis in 1985 cemented the idea in Nashville that the spectacular successes of George Strait and Ricky Skaggs were no fluke. Travis' pleasing voice, his delicate sense of humor, and his firmly traditional music combined to create a spectacularly successful string of albums, beginning with *Storms of Life*, the first debut album by a country singer to sell more than one million copies in its first year of release.

Nashville's talent scouts wasted no time scouring the countryside, roping in what came to be called the "hat acts" (because of their fondness for wearing cowboy hats). This crop of neotraditionalists includes Clint Black, Alan Jackson, Travis Tritt, and Garth Brooks, whose multimillion-selling albums have literally turned country music around. Moreover, in the process, the hats have expanded country music's audience, attracting listeners even in urban areas who are hearing pure country for the first time, and liking it.

With the arrival of the hats, country music has come full circle, losing much of its hillbilly reputation along the way. In its purest form it is a music that catalogs the most elemental saga: the journey through life by ordinary people. It is a saga as old as humankind, as relevant today as ever. Johnny Cash described his craft this way: "Country music is the heart and soul, the joy and sorrow, of the working class. It is the one voice that the working man has to express himself to the world."

Recommended Reading

Acuff, Roy, and William Neely. *Roy Acuff's Nashville: The Life and Good Times of Country Music*. New York: The Putnam Berkeley Group Inc., 1983.

Brown, Charles T. *Music U.S.A.: America's Country and Western Tradition*. New York: Prentice Hall, 1966.

Busnar, Gene. *Superstars of Country Music*. New York: J. Messner, 1984.

Cash, Johnny. *The Man in Black*. Grand Rapids, Mich.: Zondervan, 1970.

Contemporary Musicians. Gale Research, various issues.

Dellar, Fred. *The Illustrated Encyclopedia of Country Music*. New York: Harmony Books, 1977.

Grissim, John. *Country Music: White Man's Blues*. Philadelphia: Coronet Books Inc., 1970.

Haggard, Merle. *Sing Me Back Home*. New York: Times Books, 1981.

Malone, Bill. *Country Music U.S.A.*, rev. ed. Austin: University of Texas Press, 1985.

_____, and Judith McCulloh. *Stars of Country Music*. Champaign, Ill.: University of Illinois Press, 1975.

Marschall, Rick. *The Encyclopedia of Country and Western Music*. New York: Exeter Book, 1985.

McCall, Michael, David Hoekstra, and Janet Williams. *Country Music Stars: The Legends and the New Breed*. Lincolnwood, Ill.: Publications International, 1992.

McDaniel, William R., and Harold Sellgram. *Grand Ole Opry*. New York: Greenburg, 1952.

Nash, Alanna. *Behind Closed Doors: Talking With the Legends of Country Music*. New York: Knopf, 1988.

Nelson, Willie. *Willie: An Autobiography*. New York: Simon & Schuster, 1988.

Rivers, Jerry. *Hank Williams: From Life to Legend*. Muncie, Ind.: Heather Press, 1967.

Rodgers, Carrie. *My Husband—Jimmie Rogers*. Nashville: Country Music Foundation, 1975.

Sandberg, Larry, and Dick Weilssman. *The Folk Music Sourcebook*. New York: Knopf, 1976.

Shestack, Melvin. *The Country Music Encyclopedia*. New York: Crowell, 1974.

Simon, George T. *The Best of the Music Makers*. New York: Doubleday, 1979.

Stambler, Irwin, and Grelun Landon. *The Encyclopedia of Folk, Country, and Western Music*. New York: St. Martin's, 1969.

Williams, Roger M. *Sing a Sad Song: The Life of Hank Williams*. New York: Doubleday, 1970.

Recommended Listening

Bluegrass

Bill Monroe and His Blue Grass Boys. *Mule Skinner Blues*. RCA/BMG.

Country Gentleman, The. *25 Years*. Rebel.

Flatt and Scruggs. *Lester Flatt & Earl Scruggs*. Bear Family.

_____. *20 All-Time Great Recordings*. Columbia.

Flatt and Scruggs and the Foggy Mountain Boys. *Golden Hits of Flatt & Scruggs and the Foggy Mountain Boys*. Starday.

Kentucky Colonels, The. *Vintage 1965–1966*. Rounder.

Martin, Jimmy. *Jimmy Martin*. Rounder.

Monroe, Bill. *Bill Monroe 1950–1958*. Bear Family.

New Grass Revival. *Hold to a Dream*. Capitol.

Stanley Brothers. *Complete Columbia Recordings*. Bear Family.

Various artists. *The Bluegrass Compact Disc*. Rounder.

Wilma Lee and Stoney Cooper. *Sunny Side of the Mountain*. Columbia.

Country

Acuff, Roy. *Roy Acuff's Greatest Hits*, Vols. 1 and 2. Elektra.

Arnold, Eddy. *The Best of Eddy Arnold*. RCA.

Autry, Gene. *Country Music Hall of Fame*. Columbia.

Carter Family, The. *Clinch Mountain Treasures*. County.

_____. *Country Music Hall of Fame*. MCA.

Cash, Johnny. *Columbia Records 1958– 1986*. Columbia.

_____, Kris Kristofferson, Waylon Jennings, and Willie Nelson. *Highwayman I*. Columbia.

Charlie Daniels Band. *A Decade of Hits*. Epic.

Cline, Patsy. *The Patsy Cline Collection*. MCA.

Jennings, Waylon. *Music Man*. RCA.

Jones, George. *Ten Years of Hits*. Epic.

_____, and Tammy Wynette. *Greatest Hits*. RCA.

Haggard, Merle. *Best of the Best*. Capitol.

Kristofferson, Kris. *Songs of Kris Kristofferson*. Monument.

Macon, Uncle Dave. *At Home: His Last Recordings: 1950*. Bear Family.

Nelson, Willie. *Red Headed Stranger*. Columbia.

Nitty Gritty Dirt Band, The. *Will the Circle Be Unbroken*, Vol. 1. Capitol/EMI.

Parton, Dolly. *The Best of Dolly Parton*. RCA.

Robbins, Marty. *A Lifetime of Song (1951–1982)*. Columbia.

Rodgers, Jimmie. *First Sessions*. Rounder.

Skaggs, Ricky. *Don't Cheat in Our Hometown*. Epic.

Sons of the Pioneers. *Tumbling Tumbleweeds: The RCA Years*. RCA.

Travis, Randy. *Always and Forever*. Warner.

Tubb, Ernest. *Greatest Hits*. MCA.

Various artists. *60 Years of the Grand Ole Opry*. RCA.

Wells, Kitty. *Country Music Hall of Fame*. MCA.

Wills, Bob. *Anthology*. Rhino.

Photography & Illustration Credits

Index